THIRD EDITION

EXPLORING WORSHIP

A PRACTICAL GUIDE
TO PRAISE & WORSHIP

BOB SORGE

**WITH JAY THOMAS, JOSEPH ZWANZIGER,
AND BRYAN TORWALT**

Oasis House
Kansas City, Missouri

24th Printing 2021 (EW3 second printing)

Exploring Worship is also available in several languages. Visit the Translations page at www.oasishouse.com for a current listing.

If you like this book, you'll love Bob's other seminal book on worship, *FOLLOWING THE RIVER: A vision for corporate worship.* See page 239.

Unless otherwise indicated, all Scripture quotations are from the New King James Version of the Bible. Copyright © 1979, 1980, 1982, Thomas Nelson Inc., Publisher. Used by permission.

EXPLORING WORSHIP: A Practical Guide to Praise and Worship - Third Edition

Copyright © 1987, 2001, 2018 by Bob Sorge.

Published by: Oasis House
P.O. Box 522
Grandview, Missouri 64030-0522

oasishouse.com

ISBN: 978-1-937725-46-4

Cover design by Jessica Beedle

Library of Congress Cataloging-in-Publication Data
Sorge, Bob.
    Exploring worship: a practical guide to praise & worship/Bob Sorge
        p.cm. Includes bibliographical references
    ISBN: 978-1-937725-46-4 (pbk. :alk. paper)
        1. Public worship. I. Title.
    BV15.S57 2004
    264-dc22   2004041516

Stay connected please at:
YouTube.com/Bobsorge
Instagram: bob.sorge
Store: www.oasishouse.com
Blog: bobsorge.com
twitter.com/BOBSORGE
Facebook.com/BobSorgeMinistry

Who knew that Bob Sorge would take the greatest manual for praise and worship in our lifetime and make it better? That's exactly what he's done with this Third Edition of *Exploring Worship*. In a world where the modern church movement has become so focused on the *song*, Bob reminds us that it's always about the *heart*.

David Binion
Pastor, Worship Leader, Dwell Church, Dallas, TX

Bob's heart for people and for worship is on full display throughout the pages of this Third Edition. To anyone serving in worship ministry, this book is for you!

Kari Jobe Carnes
Worship Leader, Songwriter

This book is full of the practical and the profound, with biblical references throughout. I've personally made pages and pages of notes from reading this one. Every page inspires with eternal perspective on what it means to worship our amazing God!

Brian Johnson
President, Bethel Music Label, Bethel Church, Redding, CA

I'll never forget where I was, over 20 years ago, when I heard a voice whose words pierced my soul. Bob Sorge is a voice to multiple generations. Revelation and practical application are combined here, making it a must read for every leader of worship and every worshiper who wants to go deeper with God.

William McDowell
Grammy-nominated Worship Leader, Author, and Lead Pastor of Deeper Fellowship Church, Orlando, FL

As you read this new edition, you'll feel enlightened and invited into a deeper understanding of God's desire for us—which inspires us to give Him the purest and highest praise He so deserves!

Steffany Gretzinger
Songwriter, Worship Leader, Bethel Music, Redding, CA

Bob writes with great precision and wisdom—every book hits a bullseye. He carries the understanding of a true Levite. Thank you, Bob, for the heart check, head check, and hope check your books provide!

Rita Springer
Mom to Justice

Bob Sorge is one of the wisest spiritual fathers in our generation. This book is a true gift and will greatly help worship leaders, singers, and musicians.

Jon Thurlow
Worship Leader, Int'l House of Prayer, Kansas City, MO

Bob Sorge serves in a way many worship leaders and musicians ache for—an experienced mentor to sustain and guide them in their noble but demanding task.

Graham Kendrick
Worship Leader, Speaker, Recording Artist

There's so much packed into *Exploring Worship!* From the depth of theological understanding to the practical application of those truths, this book is a power-packed guide for the modern-day worshiper. Bob is an authoritative teacher and father to the worship movement today.

Thomas Miller
Executive Senior Pastor, Gateway Church, Dallas, TX

Exploring Worship is a classic, a must-have for your library.

Klaus
Pure Worship Ministries

CONTENTS

Part One: The Heart of Praise and Worship

1. **What Is Praise?** 13

    What Do We Praise? Why Should We Praise? When
    Should We Praise? Where Should We Praise? How
    Should We Praise the Lord?

2. **Entering the Presence of God** 29

    Our Approach to God's Presence; The Responsibility of
    the Individual Worshiper; The Sacrifice of Praise; The
    Cost of Praise

3. **Praise: A Weapon for Spiritual Warfare** 37

    The Scriptural Basis for Warfare Through Praise; The
    Shout in Warfare; High Praise; A Divine Assignment;
    Fight For a Release

4. **What Is Worship?** 49

    Differences Between Praise and Worship; The Essence
    of Worship; Learning to Love; The Holy Spirit and
    Worship; Worship in Spirit and Truth; Worship in
    Spirit; Worship in Truth; David Worshiped in Truth;
    Kite Metaphor; The Simplicity of Worship; The First
    Commandment in First Place

5. **Becoming a Worshiper** 73

    Worshipers are Givers; Worshipers are Passionate;
    Worshipers are Unashamed; Worshipers are
    Childlike; Worshipers are Carriers; Worship Preceded
    Forgiveness; No More Condemnation; Other
    Hindrances to Worship

6.   **The Purpose of Congregational Worship** 91

Vertical Dynamics; Horizontal Dynamics; Inward
Dynamics

7.   **Moving Prophetically in Praise and Worship** ... 109

Prophetic Worship; The Scriptural Link Between Music
and Prophecy; The Song of the Lord; Psalms, Hymns,
and Spiritual Songs; About Hymns; About Spiritual
Songs; This Is For Everyone; Take a Step of Faith; Some
Guidance

Part Two: Leading Praise and Worship

8.   **The Art of Leading Worship** 131

The Need for a Worship Leader; Qualifications of a
Worship Leader; The Leader's Musical Expertise; A
Commitment to Grow; General Guidelines for Leaders;
The Worship Leader/Musician; Invisible Leading; The
Worship Leader's Primary Objective; Getting—and
Losing—Control; The Art of Exhortation; Dealing
With Difficult Times in Worship; Standing in Worship;
Dealing With Ruts in Worship; Setting Goals for
Worship

9.   **The Worship Team** 161

The Benefits of Team Ministry; The Role of the Pastor;
The Role of the Worship Leader; The Pastor/Worship
Leader Relationship; The Role of the Chief Musician;
The Role of the Musicians; The Role of the Singers;
Sound, Media, and Screens; When to Watch for
Signals; Kinds of Signals to Use; Team Expectations;
Team Rehearsal

10. **Planning the Worship Service** 187

Navigate Uncertainty; Personal Preparation; God Uses Human Leadership; Is the Set List Sacred? Preparing a Set List; A Theme for the Service; Rut Alert; Keep Worship Fresh; Sing a New Song! Pursue New Songs; Song Elements

11. **Songwriting, by Bryan Torwalt** 205

My Journey; One Voice; Stewarding the Gift; Collaboration; Inspiration; Originality Versus Accessibility; Identity

12. **Harp and Bowl Worship, by Jaye Thomas** 215

Worship as It Is in Heaven; Worship and Intercession; Kansas City's Harp and Bowl Model

13. **Using Technology in Worship,
 by Joseph Zwanziger** 227

The Case for Technology in Worship; Benefits of Technology in Worship; Make Technology Work for You; Never Stop Learning; What about Lighting and Video? Keep the Main Thing the Main Thing

Books by Bob Sorge 238

Preface

I've undergone something few people have the privilege of experiencing: I've had a conversation with my 28-year-old self. Let me explain.

I first wrote *Exploring Worship* when I was 28 years old, and just now wrote this Third Edition 33 years later. At age 61, I'm meeting up with the 28-year-old me. While rewriting and refining the manuscript, I've had a fascinating conversation with myself in my youth.

You might ask, *What has the conversation been about?* Well, for starters, I'm struck by the zeal, strength, and insistent nature of the younger me. I'm a different man today—softened in a sweet way, I'd like to think, by the years. At the same time, I'm amazed at the Lord's grace that was on my life back then—grace to write a primer on worship that became an equipping tool for worship ministries around the world.

In 1986, *Exploring Worship* was a forerunner textbook, combining the devotional and practical aspects of praise and worship into one volume like no other book had done. Interestingly, it continues to hold that same distinction.

I've totally rewritten the book for today's worship landscape. So much has changed in 33 years! And yet the principles related to leading worship are timeless.

The goal of this book is not to answer every question a worship ministry might encounter, but to equip worship ministries to ask the right questions and then arrive together at the right answers.

Place a copy in the hands of every worship ministry member you know. Here's what readers can expect to receive:

- Glean a biblical understanding of praise and worship
- Gain the heart of a true worshiper
- Grasp the purpose of congregational worship
- Learn to flow in prophetic song
- Develop your worship leading skills
- Build a strong worship team
- Grow in songwriting
- Integrate worship with prayer

The Holy Spirit is going to keep taking us into uncharted waters. As we approach Christ's return, the glory on the church is going to grow powerfully. Get ready for another worship explosion that's about to break on the horizon. May your heart be captured by the magnificence of Jesus, and may you answer His call to "make His praise glorious" (Ps 66:2)!

Part One
The Heart of Praise and Worship

CHAPTER ONE

WHAT IS PRAISE?

Praise is the sincere, heartfelt extolling of God's person and works.

We praise all the time. We praise our children when they please us; we praise employees for a job well done; we praise dogs when they perform tricks. But in its highest expression, praise is directed toward God or expressed to others about God.

Some of the definitions given for praise in the dictionary highlight its simplicity: *to commend; to applaud; to express approval or admiration of; to extol in words or in song; to magnify; to glorify*. Notice the bi-directional focus of praise inherent in these definitions. We praise God directly by extolling Him or expressing our admiration to Him; secondly, we praise God indirectly by commending Him or magnifying Him to others.

While worship can be internal and contemplative, praise is often expressive and extroverted in nature. It's characterized by celebration and exhilaration and is expressed through singing, shouting, speaking forth, playing of musical instruments, dancing, and other external forms. To use an American idiom, praise could be defined as *raising much to-do about God*. We serve an amazing God who deserves our energetic acclamation!

Meditation is not praise. The one who ponders and contemplates the wonders of God has not yet entered into praise. To qualify as praise, thoughts must be put into action. Something must be spoken or demonstrated or it's not praise.

Someone might shut their mouth, lower their head, and say, "This is just my way of praising the Lord." But Scripture calls upon us to praise not in our "own way" but in "God's way." Furthermore, the Bible shows us that praise is to be *declared* or *manifested*. Psalm 66:8 exhorts, "Make the voice of His praise to be *heard*." Praise is not praise until it is vocalized or shown forth. In other words, it's impossible to praise with the mouth shut and the body immobile. In that posture, we might be worshiping, or meditating, or praying, or sleeping, but we are not praising.

The prophet cried, "Lift up your voice with strength, lift it up, be not afraid" (Isa 40:9). Don't be afraid to lift your voice in praise! There are both vocal and non-vocal forms of praise, but either way praise is demonstrated and observable.

Some saints might be afraid to lift their voices in the congregation for fear of being recognized as poor singers. But God's praises aren't limited to those who can sing on pitch. Even if you can't carry a tune, God's praises can be spoken. And if you can't speak, even the mute can praise God with their countenance and bodily expression.

While congregational singing provides room for many kinds of praise to be expressed simultaneously, in the final analysis, we don't praise God in our own personal way. We praise His way. He went to significant lengths, in His word, to tell us how He desires to be praised. He wants us to be sincere and authentic, but He also wants our praise to be responsive to His guidelines. So even if the lifting of hands is not "our way" of praising God, it's His way, and we should make it our own.

Praise is often an exercise of the will. Sometimes we praise Him even when we don't feel like it. Praise isn't based upon our changing feelings but His unchanging greatness. Notice how David spoke to his soul: "Bless the LORD, O my soul; and all that is within me, bless His holy name!" (Ps 103:1). When we're downcast or disengaged, sometimes we also need to talk to our souls and say, "Soul! Bless the Lord!"

"But how can I praise," someone may ask, "when I'm like this—in such a deflated emotional funk?" The Psalms help answer that question because some of them were written by men in deep emotional valleys. One psalmist described his feelings this way: "My soul is cast down within me." So he asked himself, "Why are you cast down, O my soul? And why are you disquieted within me?" Then he proceeded to take hold of himself: "Hope in God." His next statement so beautifully shows the discipline of praise: *"For I shall yet praise Him"* (Ps 42:5-6). In the same way, the Lord is pleased when we determine to praise Him regardless of our feelings and circumstances. "I *will* bless the Lord."

WHAT DO WE PRAISE?

1. His name

Praise is preoccupied with who God is and what He has done. I find that our praise of God falls into four general categories. First of all, we praise His *name*, as it says in Psalm 148:13, "Let them praise the name of the LORD, for His name alone is exalted." Psalm 34:3 says, "Let us exalt His name together." When we praise the name of the Lord, we are extolling His qualities and attributes because name represents character. Every name of God reveals something about who He is. For example, when the Lord revealed Himself as Jehovah-Jireh in Genesis 22, He was showing Himself as our Provider. We praise Him for providing all our needs. To praise His name, therefore, is to admire who God is in His many attributes. One of the best ways to grow in praise is to collect the various names of God and their meanings, because with each name your heart will thrill at the glory of who He is.

2. His word

Secondly, we praise His *word*. As David wrote, "In God (I will praise His word), in the LORD (I will praise His word), in God I have put my trust" (Ps 56:10-11). His word is true, unfailing, and revealing, and it fills us with life, wisdom, understanding, and light. When you're reading Scripture, take time to praise God for the word that's before you. He has magnified His word above all His name (Ps 138:2), so don't just praise His name; praise also His word.

3. His works

Thirdly, we praise His *works*: "One generation shall praise Your works to another" (Ps 145:4). God's works are stunning, remarkable, wondrous, and entirely unforgettable. In fact, He only does wondrous works (Ps 72:18). So if it's dull or boring, it's safe to say God didn't do it. Because all of God's works are wondrous to behold.

4. His power

Fourthly, we praise His *power*: "Be exalted, O LORD, in Your own strength! We will sing and praise Your power" (Ps 21:13). When lauding His power, we revel in the fact that nothing is impossible for Him. As Job said, He can do everything (Job 42:2).

When praising the Lord, if you ever find yourself at a loss for words, pause and think about His *name*, *word*, *works*, and *power*. Instantly, you'll find yourself filled with praise for His infinite greatness.

WHY SHOULD WE PRAISE THE LORD?

1. He commands it

First of all, we praise Him because we are commanded, "Praise the LORD!" (Ps 150:1). Have you noticed that God didn't *ask* us to praise Him? That's because kings don't ask, they command. "Why does God demand our praise?" someone might wonder. "Is He some sort of egomaniac who feeds off our adulation?" No, it's not that He needs our praises, but He knows we need to praise Him. Ultimately, praise doesn't add anything to God—but it does bring us into proper relationship with Him.

2. He loves it

A second reason for praise is because God is enthroned in our praise (see Ps 22:3). He loves our praise! It so pleases Him that He literally basks and wraps Himself in it.

3. Praise is powerful

Third, there is power in praise. When we stop striving and praise God for His mighty power, He fights for us. Praise releases His power and provision on our behalf.

4. Praise is good

We also praise God because it's "good to give thanks to the LORD" (Ps 92:1). That's because His praises are "pleasant" (Ps 135:3) and "beautiful" (Ps 33:1).

5. He's worthy of it

A fifth reason to praise God is simply because He is worthy: "You are worthy, O Lord, to receive glory and honor and power; for You created all things, and by Your will they exist and were created" (Rev 4:11). Psalm 48:1 adds, "Great is the LORD, and greatly to be praised." Consider Martin Luther's beautiful words: *A person cannot praise God only, unless he understands that there is nothing in himself worthy of praise, but that all that is worthy of praise is of God and from God. But since God is eternally praiseworthy, because He is the infinite Good and can never be exhausted, therefore they will praise Him for ever and ever.*

6. We were created for this

Sixth, we were created to praise Him. The Shorter

Catechism states, "Man's chief end is to glorify God and enjoy Him forever." Jeremiah 13:11 shows that God called the
house of Israel to Himself specifically for His praise, renown,
and glory. This is echoed in 1 Peter 2:9: "But you are a chosen
generation, a royal priesthood, a holy nation, His own special people, that you may proclaim the praises of Him who
called you out of darkness into His marvelous light." We've
been chosen for the express purpose of declaring His praises.
Isaiah capsulized this beautifully: "This people I have formed
for Myself; they shall declare My praise" (Isa 43:21).

In the search for fulfillment and significance, many look
in wrong places. Complete inner fulfillment comes only
through proper relationship with our Maker. A.W. Tozer aptly
said, *The purpose of God in sending his Son to die and live and
be at the right hand of God the Father was that He might re-
store to us the missing jewel, the jewel of worship; that we might
come back and learn to do again that which we were created to
do in the first place—worship the Lord in the beauty of holiness.*

Praise isn't a difficult and arduous task to master. Rather,
it flows naturally from our hearts when our spiritual DNA has
been encoded anew by the new birth. Praise is one of the
most natural things we do!

WHEN SHOULD WE PRAISE?

1. When we're up

We praise, first of all, when we feel like it. "Is anyone cheerful? Let him sing psalms" (Jas 5:13). When God delivered His
people by drowning Pharaoh's army in the sea, the people
of Israel erupted in praise (Ex 15). They just felt like praising
God. Praise is the perfect response when God delivers us in a
powerful way.

2. When we're down

We also praise when we don't feel like it. Praise isn't
based on our momentary emotional condition but upon His
unchanging greatness and incessant goodness. This is why

many of the Psalms offer praise to God even in the midst of great personal distress. Faith praises God's power even when it seems like His power is being withheld from us. As the psalmist said, "Why are you cast down, O my soul? And why are you disquieted within me? Hope in God, for I shall yet praise Him for the help of His countenance" (Ps 42:5).

Someone might accuse us, "Your praise is simply emotionalism!" Well, not exactly. Emotionalism is following the dictates of one's emotions. Praise is a discipline that we exercise regardless of our emotions.

While praise is not *emotionalism*, it is *emotional*. Praise *ought* to be emotional. It's the noblest way to release our God-given emotions.

3. Now

When should we praise the Lord? Now! Even when circumstances are hard or difficult. The prophet Habakkuk spoke of praising God even in the most distressing circumstances (in his case, an alien army invasion):

> Though the fig tree may not blossom, nor fruit be on the vines; though the labor of the olive may fail, and the fields yield no food; though the flock may be cut off from the fold, and there be no herd in the stalls— yet I will rejoice in the LORD, I will joy in the God of my salvation (Hab 3:17-18).

Habakkuk resolved to rejoice in the Lord even when having no food for his family. (Invasion meant economic devastation.) Why? Because he had a glimpse of God's plan to work it all out in such a good way that the blessings enjoyed afterwards would be greater than if the trial never happened.

When you get a vision of God, you can praise Him in *any* circumstance! We glorify Him because He can protect and provide in any situation.

4. At all times

When should we praise the Lord? Early in the morning, or late at night—at any time of day. David wrote, "Awake, my glory! Awake, lute and harp! I will awaken the dawn" (Ps 57:8). Psalm 119:62 says, "At midnight I will rise to give thanks to You, because of Your righteous judgments." The Levites in David's time ministered before the Lord twenty-four hours a day. These musicians "were employed in that work day and night" (1 Chr 9:33). In that same spirit, we serve the Lord as a holy priesthood and "continually offer the sacrifice of praise to God, that is, the fruit of our lips, giving thanks to His name" (Heb 13:15). The praises never stop!

The point is, we are to "bless the LORD at all times; His praise shall continually be in my mouth" (Ps 34:1). No matter when, and regardless of circumstances, it's always fitting to bless the Lord.

WHERE SHOULD WE PRAISE?

1. Around the world

Since we are to praise the Lord at all times, it follows that we should praise Him everywhere. We even praise Him in bed (Ps 149:5).

Psalm 113:3 declares, "From the rising of the sun to its going down the LORD'S name is to be praised." This means God is to be praised from dawn till dusk, but it means more than that. The sun rises in the east and sets in the west, so this verse declares that from the furthest reaches of the east to the most remote parts of the west, the name of the Lord is to be praised. He's to be praised around the entire globe!

2. In the congregation

One special place where He should be praised is the congregation of the righteous. God loves the praises of the great congregation. He loves it when the family gets together to brag on Him. Many Psalms speak of praising Him in the great assembly:

I will declare Your name to My brethren; in the midst of the assembly I will praise You... My praise shall be of You in the great assembly (Ps 22:22, 25).

LORD, I have loved the habitation of Your house, and the place where Your glory dwells... My foot stands in an even place; in the congregations I will bless the LORD (Ps 26:8, 12).

One thing I have desired of the LORD, that will I seek: That I may dwell in the house of the LORD all the days of my life, to behold the beauty of the LORD, and to inquire in His temple (Ps 27:4).

I will give You thanks in the great assembly; I will praise You among many people (Ps 35:18).

They have seen Your procession, O God, the procession of my God, my King, into the sanctuary. The singers went before, the players on instruments followed after; among them were the maidens playing timbrels. Bless God in the congregations, the Lord, from the fountain of Israel (Ps 68:24-26).

Zeal for Your house has eaten me up (Ps 69:9).

Let them exalt Him also in the assembly of the people, and praise Him in the company of the elders (Ps 107:32).

A delightful display of unity is seen when God's people lift their voices with the same melody and words at the same time in praise to God. The incense used in Moses' tabernacle was compounded from several different fragrances in order to produce what God desired. Symbolically, this shows us that the variety of praise in a congregation is very pleasing to Him. Some may be standing; others may be kneeling; some may have their hands raised; others may be dancing. This is not disorder—this is ordered unity around the greatness of our God.

3. Everywhere we go

We're called to, "Declare His glory among the nations, His wonders among all peoples" (Ps 96:3). "He has put a new song in my mouth—praise to our God; many will see it and fear, and will trust in the LORD" (Ps 40:3). God's praises are not to be confined to the ears of saints. The world needs to hear the mighty works of God and observe His glorious praises being sung. Why? Because "many will see it and fear, and will trust in the LORD" (Ps 40:3).

HOW SHOULD WE PRAISE THE LORD?

In humility, the Lord has explained to us how He wants to be praised. We don't praise Him our own private way but His way. What, then, are biblical ways to praise Him? Let's look at it.

1. Lift your hands

For starters, we *lift our hands* to Him (e.g., Neh 8:6; Ps 28:2; 63:4; 134:2; 141:2; 1 Tim 2:81). Why? It's a way to express how greatly we honor the dignity of His name. People lift their hands for many reasons. I'll mention just three.

Children lift their hands when they want to be held. For example, I remember when my son was a toddler, and how he would greet me when I came home from work. He'd meet me at the door with both arms outstretched and with a look that said, "Pick me up, Daddy!" Similarly, our upraised hands express that we want to be held by our Savior. We want His touch. We want to be carried and pulled close to His heart. Upraised arms are an expression of desire.

People lift their hands as a token of surrender. Suppose someone were to stick a revolver in your back and say, "Reach for the sky." You'd probably lift your hands. Why might a gunman demand that posture? Because it makes you defenseless. The same is true in worship. Opened arms express a lowering of defenses and an opening of our heart to the Lord. In contrast, crossed arms in worship tend to indicate a self-protective or resistant stance. By lifting our hands in worship, we express surrender to the Lord.

Football receivers are always lifting their hands. Why? It's how they catch the football that's coming their way. In other words, lifted hands are a gesture of receptivity. When we lift our hands in worship, we are expressing to the Lord that we long to receive more of His Spirit and grace.

By the way, when you lift your hands in worship, you will probably find that it helps release your heart. Try it. When you lift your hands to the Lord, you'll likely find you're not so easily distracted and your mind focuses more readily on Jesus.

2. Clap your hands

Another way the Lord invites us to praise Him is with the *clapping of hands*. Psalm 47:1 says, "Oh, clap your hands, all you peoples! Shout to God with the voice of triumph!" The idea of hand clapping in Scripture doesn't seem to be so much a "keeping of the beat" as it is the making of a great noise. David created a culture in which praise to the Lord was noisy and expressive. Let's join the clamorous acclamations! Celebrate His excellence. Be loud and jubilant in Him and clap your hands!

3. Play musical instruments

The Lord is also pleased when we *play musical instruments* to Him. Some streams in the body of Christ have insisted that musical instruments shouldn't be used in our churches, but their arguments ring hollow because the Bible is so clear about making music before the Lord. For starters, look at Psalm 150 where we're urged to praise the Lord with trumpet, lute, harp, tambourine, strings, flute, and cymbals.

4. Stand

Another way to praise is by *standing* (e.g., 2 Chron 5:12; 7:6; 29:26; Ps 135:2; Rev 4:9-11). In Moses' tabernacle, God gave instructions for many pieces of furniture to be made according to specification and placed in the tabernacle. But one piece of furniture was glaringly absent: there was no chair. The priests and Levites *stood* as they ministered to the Lord (Deut 10:8).

Standing serves two particularly strong functions in praise. First, it speaks of respect. If we were together at a meeting of dignitaries and the President of the United States walked in, we would all stand in respect. How is it, then, that when we gather together to celebrate the presence of the King of kings, we are found sitting? In the heavenly worship scene in the book of Revelation, the King is seated on the throne and all others are standing around the throne. He sits—we stand.

Second, standing indicates alertness and engagement. I find that when I sit in worship, my mind tends to relax and wander. As a more vigilant posture, standing helps us participate more intentionally in praise. I've noticed that when praise becomes vibrant people stand; and when a service begins to drag, people start to sit down. Standing and praise—they just go together.

5. Kneel, bow, fall

Kneeling, bowing, and *prostration* are also fitting expressions in praise or worship, as seen here: "Oh come, let us worship and bow down; let us kneel before the LORD our Maker" (Ps 95:6). "And the twenty-four elders and the four living creatures fell down and worshiped God who sat on the throne" (Rev 19:4). The most common posture of worship in the book of Revelation is falling in prostration. Have you ever poured out your soul to the Lord until you were leveled before Him?

6. Sing

It might be overly obvious, but *singing* is a biblical way to praise. Praises can be spoken or shouted, but most commonly they're sung. Why? Because of the beauty of music. When music is added to words of praise, something marvelous is produced that seems to be greater than the sum of the parts. It's as though the joining of words with music becomes "more" than just words and music. Our hearts engage, our souls soar, and the praises of the King arise to higher heights. This is one reason God has given us music. He knows how much it helps us in lifting our hearts in praise to Him.

7. Speak up

How does the Lord want us to praise? *Audibly!* Praise isn't praise until it's audible or manifest. We're told to, "Make the voice of His praise to be heard" (Ps 66:8). When our son Joel was being potty-trained, we used praise to show our approval and motivate him to use the potty more. If we had merely thought congratulatory thoughts and felt warm feelings but had never actually praised him, he probably would have remained in diapers a lot longer. But we chose to speak aloud our pleasure over his potty performance. Since he was eager to please, he responded favorably to our praise. The way we fussed over him, you would have thought our favorite baseball team had just won the World Series! The point here is that praise is not praise until it's expressed.

8. Dance

The Lord also revealed that He enjoys when we praise Him in *dance* (Exod 15:20-21; 2 Sam 6:14-16; Ps 30:11; 149:3; Acts 3:8). It's a way of demonstrating through bodily movement what we're feeling inside.

Dance is one of the more resisted forms of biblical praise. One pastor told me we have only one recorded incident when David danced before the Lord, and that was during the procession of the ark to Zion. It was his contention, therefore, that dancing should be a rare expression of praise in our services.

I wonder if we resist dancing before the Lord because of the humility it requires.

I realize some have problems with dance because they think it looks foolish to unbelievers and could turn them off to our services. Well, I agree, but we don't choose the ways we praise the Lord according to what outsiders approve, but according to what God approves. Our expressions of praise are not for people but for God. We allow believers to dance for joy before the Lord, not because we think it reinforces propriety, but because God has shown in His word that He delights in our abandoned praises.

Not that dancing must be a part of every service. But when a spirit of joy and celebration overtakes a congregation, don't deny them the liberty of rejoicing in the Lord and His marvelous works! We want to provide a context in which those who desire to express themselves in dance can have that liberty, while those who don't yet have that liberty feel equally free to refrain from dancing.

Those who are more expressive in their praise and worship are not "more spiritual" than those who are more reserved. Some believers who have the freedom to dance before the Lord have more problems in their lives than others with fewer freedoms. But considering all the challenges and struggles of life, sometimes the most fitting thing to do is to dance before the Lord in spite of our troubles and shortcomings. We don't rejoice because we're holier than others but because He's worthy.

Just as you don't have to be an accomplished singer to sing praises to God, you don't have to be a trained dancer to dance before the Lord. Even if you feel a little clumsy, lower your reserve and show the Lord how you feel about Him.

If you've never danced before the Lord in praise, I'd like to talk you into it. And here's why. When we initiate a physical release, it's often followed by a spiritual release. I see a hint of this principle in 1 Corinthians 15:46, "However, the spiritual is not first, but the natural, and afterward the spiritual." Sometimes a natural release comes first before a spiritual release.

Do you remember the first time you raised your hands in praise? Did you find a release in your heart when you did that? Probably so. This dynamic happens in many of the biblical forms of bodily praise. A physical action facilitates a spiritual release. And the opposite can also be true. If we're hindered in our bodily expressions, the freedom of our spirit can also be hindered.

Jesus told us to love the Lord our God with all our heart, soul, mind, and strength (Mark 12:30). Dancing is a biblical way to love the Lord with your strength. Turn on some worship music at home and dance before the Lord!

When asked why the people dance as they worship, a brother in Spain replied, "I suppose we dance because we cannot fly."

9. Shout

Shouting is also a biblical form of praise. The Scriptures exhort us to "shout to God with the voice of triumph!" (Ps 47:1). The Hebrew word *hillel*, from which we get the universal word *hallelujah*, means "to cry aloud or break out into a cry, and especially a cry of joy."

The Israelites were known by their enemies for their battle cry. When they lifted a shout, the enemy would often tremble with fear. They knew how the shout at Jericho turned that battle and caused the walls of Jericho to fall. The shout of praise triggered Israel's victory. Brothers and sisters, it's a sad day for the church when the shout of praise is no longer heard in the camp.

10. Praise in spiritual language

And finally, *speaking in tongues* is a beautiful and biblical way to praise the Lord (Acts 2:11). How deeply we cherish the precious gift of the baptism of the Holy Spirit that Jesus has given His church, together with the sign of speaking in tongues. What a beautiful release we find when we are able to express our praises to the Lord directly from our spirits unto Him! Even though some don't believe it's for today, I wish for every believer to enjoy the spiritual release that comes in magnifying God through speaking in tongues.

I suggest you sing Psalm 103:1 to the Lord, which says, "Bless the LORD, O my soul; and all that is within me, bless His holy name!" Then, as you speak those words, begin to do them. Bless Him with all that is within you. If you do, you'll likely find yourself expressing your love to the Lord through the various biblical ways mentioned in this chapter—singing, shouting, clapping hands, dancing, kneeling, bowing, prostrating, standing, and lifting of hands. He's worthy of it all!

CHAPTER TWO

ENTERING THE PRESENCE OF GOD

O We've been awakened to the beauty and glory of God in Jesus Christ, and now we naturally want to come into His presence and draw near.

When we speak of entering God's presence, we realize there are varying *manifestations* of His presence. There are at least three levels to consider. In a general sense, God is omnipresent—His presence is everywhere. So we're all in His presence, all the time. But there's more.

Second, Jesus told us that where two or three are gathered in His name, He is with them (Matt 18:20). This is a more intense manifestation of His presence.

And third, 2 Chronicles 5:13-14 gives an account of a glory cloud filling Solomon's temple when the singers and musicians lifted their praises to God. This manifestation of God's presence was so intense that the priests couldn't continue their duties. Similar dynamics still happen today. Sometimes we experience greater manifestations of His presence in worship than other times.

To come into the Lord's presence is to desire to enter into a more manifest dimension of His presence where we encounter His power and glory. Like those priests of old, we want to be so taken with God that He is all we see. Seeing Him is, after all, the supreme goal of worship.

The congregation is a place where we gather to meet with Him. As His children, we gather together in our Father's house to be with Him. What's the proper way to enter His presence as a congregation? Should we start with fast, hand-clapping praise songs, or should we come in reverence, singing slow, worshipful songs? Are there scriptural guidelines?

OUR APPROACH TO GOD'S PRESENCE

In David's time, the Israelites approached God's presence largely by songs of celebration and *praise*. We see that in these passages: "Let us come before His presence with thanksgiving; let us shout joyfully to Him with psalms" (Ps 95:2). "Serve the LORD with gladness; come before His presence with singing...Enter into His gates with thanksgiving, and into His courts with praise. Be thankful to Him, and bless His name" (Ps 100:2, 4). (See also Ps 42:4; 45:13-15; 68:24-26; Isa 30:29; 35:10.)

Other passages seem to suggest it's equally fitting to enter the Lord's house with *worship*. Consider the following passages: "Give to the LORD the glory due His name; bring an offering, and come into His courts. Oh, worship the LORD in the beauty of holiness! Tremble before Him, all the earth" (Ps 96:8-9). "But as for me, I will come into Your house in the multitude of Your mercy; in fear of You I will worship toward Your holy temple" (Ps 5:7). "Let us go into His tabernacle; let us worship at His footstool" (Ps 132:7). (See also Eccl. 5:1-2.) So which is the fitting way—*praise* or *worship*? Is there a biblical formula for starting our services?

No, there's no universal formula for entering God's presence. A service can be started with either fast songs of joyful praise or with slow songs of worship and adoration. Either approach is scriptural. If we did it the same way every time, we would lose our sense of sincerity and authenticity. To worship the Father in spirit (John 4:23-24) means we worship in the manner that most authentically engages our heart with

His. This means that worship leaders have freedom to discern for each service how the Holy Spirit would lead us into His presence.

THE RESPONSIBILITY OF THE INDIVIDUAL WORSHIPER

When we attend a corporate worship service, we want to get as much as we can out of it. We want to be edified in the Lord. And yet, our primary posture isn't that of receiving but giving. It's easy to suppose the responsibility for a worship service falls on the shoulders of those on the platform, and the rest of us have come to receive something. But the New Testament paints a different picture. We're a *royal priesthood* (1 Pet 2:9), which means all of us in the congregation are ministers to the Lord. As priests and ministers to God, therefore, each of us carries a personal responsibility to make His praises glorious.

Let's look at the personal responsibilities of each worshiper.

The first and foremost responsibility of every worshiper is to *minister to the Lord*. This responsibility to bless the Lord doesn't rest only on the pastor or the worship leader, but upon every believer in the meeting.

Each of us also has a responsibility to *prepare ourselves for worship*. We do that by spending time in prayer and the word throughout the week, and then also before the service. Sing in your car on the way to church. Staying up late Saturday night to watch a horror movie is not a good way to prepare for Sunday worship. We want to come with hearts already engaged with the Spirit of God.

A good way to prepare for worship is to *deal with any known sin* in our lives before we get to the service. If something has distanced us from the Lord, let's confess and receive His cleansing so that, when we enter the sanctuary, we're ready to give ourselves to the Lord.

When David sinned with Bathsheba, he said to the Lord, "My sin is always before me" (Ps 51:3). Whenever he tried to worship, that sin would keep flashing across his mind and hindering his confidence. That's how unconfessed sin binds us. When we confess and repent of those hindering issues, receive His gracious forgiveness, and refuse any condemnation, then we're clean and free to lift up His holy praises. Every believer has the responsibility to prepare themselves in this way for worship.

Another good way to prepare for worship is to *brighten our countenance*. Said another way, put on some spiritual makeup. For an illustration, think back to your dating days. If a young man asked you out on a date and you said yes, you probably spent a good deal of time preparing yourself. You probably primped your hair, put on makeup, and made sure you chose the right outfit. Then, when your date knocked at the door, you probably welcomed him with a warm smile and a happy voice. Even if you had a horrible day, you made the effort to look like a princess by the time he arrived.

Let's be the same way with the Lord. When we first come into His presence, let's not begin by groaning about all our complaints. Put on a garment of praise for the spirit of heaviness (Isa 61:3). (In other words, put on spiritual makeup.) Brighten up, get out your smile, lift your hands and heart, and offer thanksgiving to God.

We have a responsibility to *invest ourselves in prayer* before the service. Dr. Judson Cornwall suggested that the prayerless saint will never be a worshiper. Why not spend a few moments praying for the worship service before it starts? Jesus gave us a principle that applies here: Where your treasure is, there your heart will be (Matt 6:21). When we invest prayer for the worship service, our interest and participation go to another level.

We also need to *frequent the place of worship*. We're exhorted to not neglect the assembly of the saints (Heb 10:25). When a congregation gathers to worship, they're making a statement in their community, in the presence of demonic powers, and before heaven. It's a place where the life of God flows between all the members of the body of Christ. How can a member that cuts itself off from the body remain alive?

✱ When we come into the presence of God, we should *bring an offering.* We come not as beggars but as givers. Psalm 96:8 says, "Bring an offering, and come into His courts." Rather than coming to see how much we can receive, let's press in to see how much of ourselves we can give to Him. Come with a financial offering, and also come with an offering of the heart. And be ready to reach out in care to other brothers and sisters as a need becomes evident. God isn't trying to grow lazy leeches who know how to sponge off the pastor and the congregation. He loves cheerful givers—who come to the congregation with a heart to contribute something.

Psalm 66:2 gives us a marvelous mandate: "Make His praise glorious." That requires us to *invest energy.* Corporate praise is not automatically glorious. We must make it glorious. Come prepared to throw your heart and soul—all your energies—into the worship service. Glorious praises are found by those who make them so. We serve a great God, and He deserves praise in accordance with His greatness. He deserves the most lavish fanfare we can muster. Praise isn't the response of those who have passively waited for some heavenly shower; it's initiated by those who accept their responsibility to make something of His praises.

Investing energy into the worship service means we worship wholeheartedly even when our strength is small. When we're tired, we don't wait for something to happen in the meeting that inspires our enthusiasm. We give our love to the Lord, even when a service seems to lack spontaneous surges. Sometimes worship demands discipline. We don't worship only when a song manages to hit our buttons.

When you scratch a dog in the right place, sometimes it automatically flails its paw in response. As worshipers, we don't want to be like that dog, waiting for the worship leader to scratch us in just the right place so we can reflexively worship. Rather, we want to give ourselves to the Lord in a way that's self-motivated and giving of our energies.

Furthermore, let's be eager to *enter quickly* into God's presence. When Jesus called His disciples "slow of heart"

(Luke 24:25), it wasn't exactly complimentary. Let's not be slow of heart when it comes to praise and worship, but eager to enter in with the very first song.

Resolve to *push aside distractions* when coming into the Lord's presence. One of the biggest distractions can be all the human dynamics happening in the meeting. We see something and thoughts start to go off in our heads like popcorn. "The worship leader must be having a bad day." "What's the pastor doing? He doesn't look like he's worshiping at all." "Oops, that was a bad chord on the guitar." "The drummer needs to speed it up, this song is dragging." "That couple over there looks like they had a fight on the way to church today." "It doesn't seem like anybody is into this song." "Why is that family fifteen minutes late every week?"

We may even feel that we're being especially discerning. "The problem is, the worship team hasn't invested prayer into this service." We may be accurate in identifying human weaknesses—that the worship leader's intonation is flat, or that the keyboardist doesn't know the chords to the song, or that the drummer is overbearing. But were we so distracted we never even worshiped? Let's refuse to be robbed by the human distractions around us. David said, "I will bless the LORD at all times" (Ps 34:1)—even when the guitarist can't get the attention of the sound team, no matter how large she waves her hands. Tune out the distractions and set your eyes on the Lord.

● We have a responsibility to *be worshipers all week long.* True worship isn't just a Sunday morning event but a way of life. All of life is a 24/7 praise to God. When those who have been worshiping all week assemble, the atmosphere is combustible. The goal of worship leaders, therefore, is not simply to cultivate thirty minutes of exuberant worship on Sunday mornings but to cultivate worshipers who live a life of praise all week long. I see a difference between someone who worships and someone who is a worshiper. Some people worship when they come to church, but worshipers worship all week long—in all their activities and relationships.

When I say worshipers worship all week long, I'm not suggesting they're perfect. I'm just saying they've resolved to stay in the perfecting process of Romans 12:1-2.

> I beseech you therefore, brethren, by the mercies of God, that you present your bodies a living sacrifice, holy, acceptable to God, which is your reasonable service. And do not be conformed to this world, but be transformed by the renewing of your mind, that you may prove what is that good and acceptable and perfect will of God.

THE SACRIFICE OF PRAISE

Scripture speaks twice of offering a *sacrifice of praise* to God:

- Bring the sacrifice of praise into the house of the LORD (Jer 33:11).

- Therefore by Him let us continually offer the sacrifice of praise to God, that is, the fruit of our lips, giving thanks to His name (Heb 13:15).

The idea here is that praise is not always something we feel like offering. Sometimes, if it's to happen, it requires a selfless sacrifice on our part.

We all love those times when we feel like praising the Lord. But sometimes it's the last thing we want to do. But God is worthy of our praise, even when our souls are disengaged or downcast. What do you do when your soul is downcast? You offer up *a sacrifice of praise.*

Sacrifice reminds us of the animal sacrifices the Old Covenant required. But now, instead of a burnt animal, God delights in the sacrifices of a burning heart.

A sacrifice speaks of something costly, the giving of something that is dear to us. This is illustrated beautifully in 1 Chronicles 21. David wanted to offer a sacrifice to God on

Ornan's threshing floor, so Ornan offered to give David the land, the oxen for burnt offerings, the wood, and the wheat for the grain offering. But David refused. He said, "No, but I will surely buy it for the full price, for I will not take what is yours for the LORD, nor offer burnt offerings with that which costs me nothing" (1 Chr 21:24). He paid six hundred pieces of gold to Ornan for his property so that the offering would be a *sacrifice.*

It's not a sacrifice until it costs us something.

Sometimes our praises are most meaningful to God when we least feel like offering them. Because it means we're sacrificing.

THE COST OF PRAISE

Praise is not always easy and free. Sometimes it's offered at a price. First, there's the cost of energy. Sometimes, when we come to the congregation, we're weary and ready to relax. We don't always feel like lifting our hands to the Lord or standing through an entire worship service. That's precisely the time, however, when we have opportunity to offer up a true sacrifice of our energy and bless the Lord with our heart, soul, mind, and strength.

Then there's the cost of preparation. When we know we're gathering to the place of praise, sometimes we realize we need to prepare our hearts through cleansing, confession, repentance, and consecration.

Third, there's the cost of time. Sometimes time is our most precious commodity of the day. Ask me for twenty dollars and I'll give it rather easily. But ask me for two hours of my time? That's much more precious and harder to give. But entering into God's presence will inevitably require a sacrifice of time. Sometimes we need to stop everything and just devote ourselves to intimate communion with the Lord. Just as it takes more than five minutes to have a meaningful interaction with a friend or spouse, fulfilling communion with Jesus will cost us time.

CHAPTER THREE

PRAISE: A WEAPON FOR SPIRITUAL WARFARE

We're in a war. Paul told us that we fight, not with human forces, but with demonic principalities, powers, and rulers in heavenly places (Eph 6:12). Furthermore, he enjoined us to clothe ourselves with the armor of God so we might effectively withstand the attacks of the evil one (Ephesians 6:10-18). The war is intense and real.

Spiritual victories are won through many means such as intercessory prayer, the name of Jesus, the confession of God's word, and the blood of Christ. To that list we add praise. Praise is a form of spiritual warfare for overcoming the schemes of the enemy.

THE SCRIPTURAL BASIS FOR WARFARE THROUGH PRAISE

Corporate worship is an assault on the gates of hell. Private praise is also combative. Praise can be seen as a militant activity in Scripture, going all the way back to the Israelites' crossing of the Red Sea. Egypt's army had just drowned in the rushing waters, and the people of God were safe on the other side. Miriam grabbed a tambourine and

led the women in singing, "Sing to the LORD, for He has tri-
umphed gloriously! The horse and its rider He has thrown
into the sea!" (Exod 15:21). On that occasion, Moses and all
Israel sang a triumphal song of victory before the Lord and
celebrated with this declaration: "The LORD is a man of war:
the LORD is his name" (Exod 15:3). After seeing how God
dealt with Pharaoh and his armies, they knew they had wit-
nessed a great battle strategist in action.

The Lord revealed Himself as a warrior to Joshua. As
Joshua was about to lead Israel across the Jordan River into
Canaan, a Man appeared to him with a drawn sword. Joshua
asked Him, "Are you for us or for our enemies?" "Neither," He
replied, "but as commander of the army of the LORD I have
now come" (Josh 5:13-14). Jesus had come—the Commander
of heaven's armies—to lead Israel in combat against the enemies of God in Canaan.

Yes, Jesus is our tender and compassionate Savior,
healer, and friend. But He's more than that. He's also the
Commander-in-Chief of heaven's hosts. He's the same yesterday, today, and forever, so He's still our military captain
(Heb 2:10). As long as His enemy is loose and active in the
earth, God will be known and experienced as a warrior.

JEHOSHAPHAT'S CHOIR

The Bible has some marvelous stories of God accom-
plishing great victories for His people in response to their
praise. One of the foremost instances was in the days of King
Jehoshaphat when the Edomites arose to invade Judah (2
Chr 20). Alarmed, Jehoshaphat gathered all of Judah to the
temple to seek the Lord. In his prayer he confessed, "For we
have no power against this great multitude that is coming
against us; nor do we know what to do, but our eyes are upon
You" (v. 12). In response, the Spirit of God came upon a Levite
named Jahaziel, a descendant of Asaph (the chief musician
at the time of King David). Jahaziel proclaimed, "Do not be
afraid nor dismayed because of this great multitude, for the
battle is not yours, but God's" (v. 15). The Lord spoke clearly

through Jahaziel, "You will not need to fight in this battle. Position yourselves, stand still and see the salvation of the LORD, who is with you, O Judah and Jerusalem!" (v. 17).

In response Jehoshaphat stood and said, "Hear me, O Judah and you inhabitants of Jerusalem: Believe in the LORD your God, and you shall be established; believe His prophets, and you shall prosper." The citation for that verse is 2 Chronicles 20:20, and so I say with a smile that that verse helps to give me 20-20 vision on spiritual realities.

I imagine Jehoshaphat musing on Jehaziel's prophecy, "This is God's battle. We don't need to fight. We just need to stand and watch the salvation of God. Well, since that's the case, let's mobilize the praise choir!"

The biblical account says that Jehoshaphat appointed a group of praisers to go out in front of the army to offer thanks and praise to God for the victory they didn't yet have.

Just think about it. Jehoshaphat was being invaded by alien hordes, so he gathered his army according to ranks. Then he basically said, "Okay, now we need some singers." With his army on one side, he gathered a choir of praisers on the other side. Then he did something ludicrous. He told the singers to move out first, get in front of the army, and lead the soldiers into battle—singing praises the whole way! He made the choir the vanguard. He knew who his true warriors would be that day—the praisers would call the win.

This was bold faith. Jehoshaphat believed that if God's promises were true, then all they needed to do was offer up praises and thanksgiving to God and watch Him fight for them. The men in the choir must have shared Jehoshaphat's bold faith because they made themselves the first line of defense against the enemy.

Off they went to war, with the choir singing and the army following. My, how they must have sung! They praised the beauty of holiness, saying, "Praise the LORD, for His mercy endures forever" (v. 21).

What happened next? The text tells us.

Now when they began to sing and to praise, the
LORD set ambushes against the people of Ammon,
Moab, and Mount Seir, who had come against Judah;
and they were defeated. For the people of Ammon
and Moab stood up against the inhabitants of Mount
Seir to utterly kill and destroy them. And when they
had made an end of the inhabitants of Seir, they
helped to destroy one another. So when Judah came
to a place overlooking the wilderness, they looked
toward the multitude; and there were their dead
bodies, fallen on the earth. No one had escaped.
When Jehoshaphat and his people came to take
away their spoil, they found among them an abun-
dance of valuables on the dead bodies, and precious
jewelry, which they stripped off for themselves, more
than they could carry away; and they were three
days gathering the spoil because there was so much
(2 Chr 20:22-25).

I imagine Jehoshaphat's soldiers looking at one another,
glancing down a bit sheepishly at their swords and spears,
shrugging, putting down their weapons, and sauntering in to
clean up the plunder. The real warriors on that occasion were
not the soldiers in the army but the singers in the choir. As
they sang praises to God, He fought for them, and the soldiers
didn't even have to lift a finger (except to gather plunder).
What an awesome victory!

Look again at their lyrics: "Praise the LORD, for His mercy endures forever" (v. 21). On the surface, the song didn't
seem very militant. They weren't calling down fire or invok-
ing God's wrath or cursing their enemies. They didn't even
address their enemies. Rather, their focus was on God's
promise and power to make good on it. They were thanking
and praising Him for mercifully delivering them from the enemy, even before the deliverance had happened. With their
faith-filled praise, they released God to act according to His
wisdom and power. They weren't telling God how to defeat

the enemy, they were just praising Him because they knew He would.

Warfare through praise doesn't have to tell God what to do—it praises Him for His wisdom and might, recognizing that He's capable of settling the problem in a way that glorifies His name. It doesn't focus on the battle or the enemy; it looks only to the solution—God! "But the people who know their God shall be strong, and do great exploits" (Dan 11:32).

THE PHILIPPIAN JAIL BREAK

Another famous instance of warfare through praise is found in Acts 16. Paul and Silas were heavily flogged in Philippi and then put in stocks in the city jail. Not only were their bodies throbbing from the beating, but the stocks were designed to add to their misery. What do you do when you're in jail and in too much pain to sleep? Paul and Silas were like, "If you can't sleep, then praise God!"

Unable to find a comfortable position, they began to lift their voices in praise and thanksgiving to God. And they didn't hold back. Midnight is a good time for prisoners to sing praises to God! They sang so loudly that all the prisoners in the jail could hear them. They were advertising the goodness of God in a context where no one could see any of His goodness.

They weren't asking God for deliverance. They didn't call for judgment on the city that had mistreated them. They didn't rebuke the devil or curse the jailer. They simply praised God for His greatness and goodness. They had no idea God was about to open the prison, so they weren't praising in order to stimulate a divine response. They were offering up thanks at a time when it seemed they'd be spending the whole night in the stocks.

But God liked their style. He refused to let their praises go unanswered. What happened? "Suddenly there was a great earthquake, so that the foundations of the prison were shaken; and immediately all the doors were opened and everyone's chains were loosed" (Acts 16:26). The story ends with the jailer and his entire household confessing faith in Christ and getting baptized. When God responded to their praise, not only were Paul and Silas freed from their chains, but an entire family was delivered from the clutches of Satan. Praise is powerful!

THE SHOUT IN WARFARE

The shout of praise was instrumental in bringing victory in several biblical stories. For example, the people of Israel used a shout of praise to overcome the city of Jericho. For six days they tramped around the city, walking the entire circumference of the city each morning. On the seventh day, they arose early to march around the city seven times. Here's the battle plan God gave Joshua: After the seventh time around the city, the trumpeters were to sound and then the people were to lift a shout.

What happened? "So the people shouted when the priests blew the trumpets. And it happened when the people heard the sound of the trumpet, and the people shouted with a great shout, that the wall fell down flat. Then the people went up into the city, every man straight before him, and they took the city" (Josh 6:20).

Did their shout hit the resonant frequency of Jericho's walls, causing the walls to collapse? No, God acted on their behalf. Jesus and His angels were present, fighting for Israel. Israel did their part by obediently offering a great shout of praise, and then God did His part by granting them a supernatural victory.

For a second example, let me remind you of Gideon's story. He's the guy who had the shrinking army. He started with a mere 32,000 soldiers, which seemed so small to Gideon in contrast to the size of the enemy's armies, but to God the army was too large. So God reduced them to 10,000 warriors. But that was still too large for God. He said to Gideon, "The people who are with you are too many for Me to give the Midianites into their hands, lest Israel claim glory for itself against Me, saying, 'My own hand has saved me'" (Judg 7:2).

So God whittled his numbers down again until he had only 300 soldiers left. Gideon was to take on the entire Midianite army with just 300 men.

God gave Gideon the battle strategy. His 300 men were to surround the Midianite camp, placing a sizable distance between each other. At Gideon's signal, they were to blow a trumpet, break the jar hiding their torch, lift up their torch, and then shout, "The sword of the LORD and of Gideon!" (Judg 7:20).

What happened? Well, in response to their shout, the Lord fought for Israel. He caused the Midianite army to turn on itself and kill one another. Israel enjoyed a mighty victory that day because they obediently lifted a shout of praise in the time and way God specified.

I relish moments of silent reverence as we stand in awe before God's beautiful holiness, but there's a time when silence is inappropriate. There comes a time to shout. It's a sad day for the church when the shout is gone from the camp.

I believe God wants to show us how to use the shout of praise as a spiritual weapon today. We should wait for His timing and strategy. Yes, we should war in intercession. But then there comes a time to stop petitioning, and simply rejoice in the power of our sovereign Savior. He is Lord over every dilemma. When we rejoice in His strength, He goes to battle. We praise; He fights. As the Spirit directs our praises, our faith begins to rise to the level of our confession, and God responds to our faith and obedience. I imagine Him thinking, "Wow, My children actually believe that I'm in charge of this situation. Look at them! They're rejoicing in My strength and power even in the middle of their crisis." How can He do anything but respond to such simple, bold faith?

RESTING IN OUR WARRIOR

Sometimes the Spirit will lead us to become militant in praise, but praise in spiritual warfare is not always militant. Sometimes it's expressed in peace and trust. We're not the ones being militant, God is. If there's any fighting to be done,

let God do it. We don't pretend to have power over the enemy in ourselves, but we do rejoice in the God who does.

Here's a few more Scriptures that point to the way praise
can be a weapon to release God's power:

> "When you go to war in your land against the enemy
> who oppresses you, then you shall sound an alarm
> with the trumpets, and you will be remembered be-
> fore the LORD your God, and you will be saved from
> your enemies" (Num 10:9). (God said that in response
> to the trumpet blast of praise He would save them.)

> "Judah, you are he whom your brothers shall praise;
> your hand shall be on the neck of your enemies" (Gen
> 49:8). (Judah's name means "Praise." Jacob declared
> that the hand of the "praisers" will be on the neck of
> their enemies.)

> Out of the mouth of babes and nursing infants You
> have ordained strength, because of Your enemies,
> that You may silence the enemy and the avenger (Ps
> 8:2). (Jesus showed in Matthew 21:16 that David was
> referring to praise coming from babes. God in his wis-
> dom has determined to have praise come from those
> with no battle experience! Young children are utterly
> naive when it comes to fighting battles the world's
> way, but they are childlike enough to lift their voices
> in praise to the God who fights for them.)

> Let the high praises of God be in their mouth, and
> a two-edged sword in their hand, to execute ven-
> geance on the nations, and punishments on the peo-
> ples; to bind their kings with chains, and their nobles
> with fetters of iron; to execute on them the written
> judgment—this honor have all His saints. Praise the
> LORD! (Ps 149:6-9). (God has given us a twofold com-
> bination with which to defeat our enemies: the high

praise of God in our mouths and the word of God in our hands.)

HIGH PRAISE

Psalm 149:6 refers to *high* praise. Let me suggest a few things I think that means.

Praise can be *high* in volume. Sometimes it's fitting for our praises to be loud.

Praise can be *high* in intensity. In corporate worship, sometimes we're aware that the intensity of praise grows as the service progresses because the worshipers become more engaged and proactive in the praise service.

Praise can be *high* in timbre. In other words, it can be sung at the higher registers of our voice's potential.

Praise can be *high* as descriptive of the praise around the throne of God. High in the heavens, cherubim and seraphim and angels and creatures and saints are lifting their voices in praise of God's holiness. I believe it's possible for us, here below, to mirror their praise. Heaven and earth become something like an antiphonal choir. Heaven's choir sings praises to the Lamb, and then earth's choir echoes their response. When we share in the spirit of praise that surrounds the throne, our praise is truly *high*—on earth as it is in heaven.

Finally, praise can be *high* when it ascends into the heavens and wars on our behalf. We recognize that spiritual forces of wickedness function in heavenly realms (Eph 6:12). Daniel 10 seems to indicate evil powers hover over nations, cities, households, and individuals. One of the ways we resist the powers of darkness is through high praise.

Psalm 149 links high praise with a two-edged sword, which seems to point to God's word. There is a beautiful relationship between the singing of God's praise and the preaching and singing of the word. Coupling the praises of God with the authoritative preaching of God's word produces a powerful combination. When churches join high praise with the proclamation of God's word, the kingdom of God moves forward militantly against the powers of darkness.

We can see how this happened on the day of Pentecost. When the Holy Spirit was poured out on the church in Acts 2, they entered into high praise. God-fearing Jews from many nations were in Jerusalem and heard the Christians speaking in other tongues and declaring the wonderful works of God. After their *high praise,* Peter's sermon cut like a *two-edged sword,* and about three thousand people repented and came to Christ. Praise and preaching produced a strong harvest.

In Isaiah 30:32, the Lord indicated He would judge Israel's oppressor, Assyria, to the accompaniment of musical instruments: "And in every place where the staff of punishment passes, which the LORD lays on him, it will be with tambourines and harps; and in battles of brandishing He will fight with it." There's a time, in spiritual warfare, for instruments to get involved. Get out the tambourine! Get out the guitar! Let the keyboardists sit down, and let the percussionists take their place. It's time to go to war! When the time is right, the Lord will empower a worship ministry to lead the charge in high praise. And God will punish the enemy.

God wants to punish the kingdom of darkness by rescuing from Satan's hand souls who are bound in iniquity. Every time a soul is snatched from darkness and brought into God's kingdom, the purposes of Satan are frustrated, a multitude of sins are covered, and a newly born saint emerges. Have you been praying for your unbelieving spouse? To your intercessions add praise. Rejoice in God's power and release Him to fight on your behalf.

Some young people who have participated in Youth With A Mission (a worldwide missions organization) told me that they have experienced times when their personal evangelism seemed to be hitting a brick wall. At such times, they would get out the guitars and start singing the praise of God wherever they were. The spiritual walls would begin to crumble, and they would have a breakthrough at that locality.

A DIVINE ASSIGNMENT

We go to war through praise only through the specific

leading of the Holy Spirit. He can prompt you quietly in your own heart regarding a situation in your life. And He can bring direction to a corporate worship service through the leaders who are present. For instance, in the middle of a service, a church elder might sense in the Holy Spirit that the church is to go to war in a corporate way. Perhaps a family in the church has been under attack from the evil one. Or perhaps God is highlighting a certain Scripture to the entire congregation. With the help of the musicians and singers, the congregation can lift their hearts in praise. When we respond to the Holy Spirit's leading in this way, God delights to respond to our praise.

In the story of Jehoshaphat that we covered earlier (2 Chr 20), the people received a very specific word from God. All they had to do was praise in obedience and faith.

When we attempt to engage in spiritual warfare without a word from God, we can hit into some negatives. If God is not in it, our warring praises can be a clanging cymbal, a beating of the air, a phantom battle. Furthermore, if we attempt to tackle an assignment God is not actually giving us, we can end up suffering a setback unnecessarily. But when God gives a directive to take on a certain stronghold, and we are careful to follow His lead, we will be amazed as we watch God at work.

FIGHT FOR A RELEASE

Sometimes when God's people gather for corporate worship, it can feel as if there's spiritual resistance in the room to the spirit of praise. It's almost as though spiritual forces are hindering the praise. It's tempting for worship leaders to wonder if their enemy is the congregation itself. They feel that the people almost fight their attempts to arise in praise. And in some cases, that might actually be happening. For a dozen or more reasons, a congregation can harden themselves against the attempts of the worship ministry to lead them. Worship leaders often ask, "What can we do when there is a sense of heaviness in the congregation, as though spiritual forces are holding the people back from entering into that which their hearts truly desire?"

Sometimes the answer is, go to war. For example, a worship ministry might gather on Saturday night and battle together on behalf of the next day's service. Or the worship team might find themselves pressing forward militantly right in the middle of a worship service. When the response of the people might tempt us to turn back, the Holy Spirit might urge us to press forward. Sometimes we don't find a full release in corporate worship because we back off too soon.

Don't relent until the Lord gives a release of praise in the congregation, even if it takes weeks or months. Go to war until you find that release, and then when you find it, lift high the praises of the King!

CHAPTER 4

WHAT IS WORSHIP?

Finding the perfect definition for worship can be a little elusive. Perhaps that's because worship is a matter of the heart, and every attempt to define the heart can feel inadequate. Praise seems rather straightforward to identify, but worship is another matter. Being a heart encounter, worship is as infinite in its depths as God's heart and those of His worshipers.

At one time, I collected several definitions of worship. Though these are but attempts to put into words what essentially is a feeling, perhaps they can help us begin to understand something of the basic nature of worship.

1. Worship is conversation between God and man, a dialogue that should go on constantly in the life of a Christian.

2. Worship is giving to God and involves a lifetime of giving to Him the sacrifice He asks for—our total selves.

3. Worship is our affirmative response to the self-revelation of the triune God. For the Christian, each act of life is an act of worship when it is done with love that responds to the Father's love. Living should be

constant worshiping, since worship may be said to provide the metabolism for spiritual life.

4. Worship was the outcome of the fellowship of love between the Creator and man and is the highest point man can reach in response to the love of God. It's the first and principal purpose of man's eternal calling.

5. Worship is one's heart expression of love, adoration, and praise to God with an attitude and acknowledgment of His supremacy and Lordship.

6. Worship is an act by a redeemed man, the creature, toward God, his Creator, whereby his will, intellect, and emotions gratefully respond in reverence, honor, and devotion to the revelation of God's person expressed in the redemptive work of Jesus Christ, as the Holy Spirit illuminates God's written word to his heart.

7. Worship means "to feel in the heart." Worship also means to express in some appropriate manner what we feel.

8. True worship and praise are "awesome wonder and overpowering love" in the presence of our God.

9. Worship is the ability to magnify God with our whole being—body, soul, and spirit.

10. The heart of true worship is the unashamed pouring out of our inner self upon the Lord Jesus Christ in affectionate devotion.

11. Worship is fundamentally God's Spirit within us contacting the Spirit in the Godhead.

12. Worship is the response of God's Spirit in us to that Spirit in Him whereby we answer, "Abba, Father," deep calling unto deep.

13. Worship is the ideally normal attitude of a rational creature properly related to the Creator.

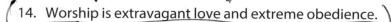

(14. Worship is extravagant love and extreme obedience.)

Each definition, while insightful, somehow seems to fall short. I once heard my father-in-law, Morris Smith, say, "Real worship defies definition; it can only be experienced." I think that's right, for worship was never intended by God to be the discussion of textbooks but rather the communion with God experienced by His loved ones.

Worship is not a musical activity but an expression of the heart. Music can aid worship, but it isn't necessary for worship. Worship isn't an activity simply for those who love to sing. Thousands of folks who "can't carry a tune in a bucket" are adoring worshipers. Music can be used as a catalyst for worship, but even when no musical instruments are available, like the woman in Luke 7, we can anoint the feet of Jesus with the oil of our affections.

DIFFERENCES BETWEEN PRAISE AND WORSHIP

Perhaps we can understand worship better if we can distinguish it from praise. Distinguishing the two is not so easy, and even possibly artificial. "Praise and worship" are sometimes spoken in the same breath, and it's possible to do both simultaneously. But often they operate differently.

In a corporate gathering, one person might be worshiping while another is praising. Looking at them both, it may appear to you that they're both involved in the same activity. Sometimes the differences are subtle. The outward forms that praise and worship employ are often identical.

Discerning between the two can be almost as difficult as dividing between soul and spirit. There's only one thing sharp enough to discern between soul and spirit, and that is the word of God (Heb 4:12). If I try to distinguish between my own soul and spirit, the lines become very blurry. Similarly, while praise and worship are different entities, they are often impossible to separate.

The four expressions known as prayer, thanksgiving, praise, and worship are very closely related. Areas within these expressions overlap each other. The diagram below is my attempt to show how these four areas overlap, and thus are sometimes difficult to completely separate from each other.

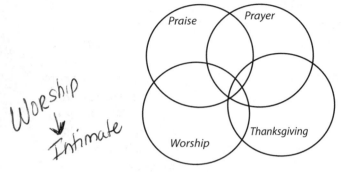

The differences between praise and worship in this chapter, therefore, are almost hypothetical. But perhaps we'll gain a better grasp of worship by considering these hypothetical differences.

First, God doesn't need our praises, but He does seek worshipers. Let me explain the difference. He commands our praise, not because He needs it, but because we need to praise Him. It positions us rightly before Him and changes us. We humble ourselves so we can exalt Him. Thus, praise places us in proper relationship to God. God doesn't really need our praises, but it seems to be different when it comes to worship. There's something about worship that He desires and wants. Jesus said that the Father *seeks* worshipers (John 4:23). He seeks them because He longs for their hearts.

Notice that God seeks *worshipers*, not *worship*. He's not after the verbiage of worship, but rather the wholehearted affections of true worshipers. He seeks the heart.

A second distinctive between the two is that praise can sometimes be distant while worship is usually intimate. The heart of man need not be near to God for praise to occur. I have heard stories of people who have sung and praised God while in a drunken state. I have even heard of drunkards witnessing to one another and in their witness giving praise to God. On one occasion, Jesus said the rocks would cry out if His disciples didn't praise Him (Luke 19:37-40). Rocks obviously don't have an interactive relationship with the Lord, and yet it's possible for them to praise. The trees, the mountains, rivers, sun, moon, and stars—all can praise the Lord (Ps 148:3-12), and yet God has no reciprocal relationship with any of these. So praise can happen from a distance, and without relationship.

Worship is different. It happens in the nearness of heartfelt relationship. In worship, we "kiss the Son" (Ps 2:12). It requires relationship because it involves both giving and receiving. Praise can function like a one-way street, but worship is two-way communion and fellowship.

Third, praise is always seen or heard, but worship isn't always evident to an observer. Sometimes worship is visible and obvious, but at other times it's quiet and visually imperceptible. Only God knows when someone is worshiping.

Fourth, praise has a strong horizontal dynamic to it, while worship is primarily vertical. Let me explain. In praise, we often speak to one another of His goodness and greatness (Eph 5:19). Praise is very aware of other praisers in the room. In worship, however, we lose sight of others around us and become preoccupied with the wonder of who He is.

Praise is often preparatory to worship. We might come initially into His presence with thanksgiving and praise (Ps 100:4), but that often morphs naturally into worship. Praise often acts as a gateway to worship. But to say praise starts first and worship comes next is not a hard and fast rule. In some meetings, a depth of worship can explode in the end with exuberant praise. Praise and worship, therefore, are beyond any kind of a confining formula.

Another distinction between praise and worship is often found in the mood of the music. Worship is often accompanied by slower songs and praise by faster songs. I say *often*, but not *always*, because exceptions abound. But in the main, it seems the mood of slower music is more conducive to worship, while the mood of faster music more readily supports praise. Ultimately, the best way to determine whether a song is a "praise song" or a "worship song" is to examine the lyrics.

A final variance between praise and worship is seen in the way praise is often accompanied by effort while worship is usually effortless. Chapter one dealt with the aggressive nature of praise. A dynamic praise service can leave you sweating. But worship seems to operate differently, carried along by the power of the Holy Spirit.

I'm not implying that worship is superior to praise. Both are beautiful and valuable, and both play a vital role in the life of every believer and congregation. If we think worship is more desirable than praise, the push will be on in every praise service to progress into worship. But praise is a glorious end all in itself. Sometimes the Holy Spirit will lead us to remain in praise for a protracted period of time because that is what He is empowering in the moment.

I've actually heard people speak disparagingly of praise songs. I've heard comments like, "I'm not interested in songs that speak *about* God, I only want songs that speak *to* God. Let's go vertical!" I agree that most of our worship should be a vertical encounter with God, but that doesn't negate the wonderful and desirable role of praise. Paul spoke of both dynamics when he wrote of, "speaking to one another in psalms and hymns and spiritual songs, singing and making melody in your heart to the Lord" (Eph 5:19). In that verse, he has us speaking "to one another" and also "to the Lord." Speaking to one another in song is biblical. I don't think we should be overly analytical about whether a song is addressing God in the first, second, or third person. Let's get our eyes off the mechanics and be childlike in engaging with Jesus. Whether the song is vertical or horizontal, let's give our hearts fully to the Lord!

THE ESSENCE OF WORSHIP

When I want to consider the foundational essence of worship, I go back to the two men in the Bible who first introduced this topic to us: Job and Abraham. Let's start with Job.

The book of Job is the first Bible book ever put on paper. Its existence predates even Genesis. Therefore, it rightly contains the first reference to worship in Scripture. Let me remind you about his story.

Incredible calamity hit Job in one single day. He lost his camels, donkeys, oxen, sheep, and servants—in other words, his source of livelihood. And then, on the same day, he lost all ten of his children (a tornado caused the house to collapse on all of his children during a festive party). Job's response is gripping: "Then Job arose, tore his robe, and shaved his head; and he fell to the ground and worshiped" (Job 1:20).

If we agree this is the first mention of worship in the Bible, then we can say worship is what we do in the face of great tragedy and personal trials. Worship at its essence is not what we do when life is happy and we feel blessed; it's what we do when we lose things that are most dear to us.

The test of worship is not on Sunday morning. When we gather with God's people on Sunday morning, it's easy to worship. The saints are gathered in holy convocation; the psalmists have prayed and prepared and are ready to lead; the song of the Lord begins to arise; the presence of God fills the house. If you can't worship on Sunday morning, you're probably dead.

The test of worship doesn't happen on Sunday morning. It happens on Monday morning—when you go to work with those uncircumcised Philistines.

The test of worship happens when the bottom falls out from beneath us, when life careens out of control, when our pain levels hit the ceiling, and we have no idea what is happening to us. That's the time when we discover whether we have the heart of Job, who said, "The LORD gave, and the LORD has taken away; blessed be the name of the LORD" (Job 1:21).

Worship acknowledges His Lordship in the face of life-shattering circumstances. When everything that surrounds one's life screams, "God is unjust! He doesn't love me! He has forsaken me," the true worshiper says, "The Lord is good. Blessed be the name of the Lord." The bottom line on worship is loving the Lord in the midst of our greatest losses.

The second mention of worship in the Bible occurs in Abraham's story. God spoke audibly to Abraham, instructing him to take his only, beloved son Isaac, and sacrifice him to God on a certain mountain. Abraham arose immediately, packed the necessary things, and hit the road with Isaac and two young men.

When the Lord's mountain finally came into view, notice what Abraham said to the servants: "Stay here with the donkey; the lad and I will go yonder and worship, and we will come back to you" (Gen 22:5).

What did worship mean for Abraham on this occasion? It meant building an altar, tying his son, placing his son on the altar, lifting the knife, plunging it through his son's heart, and then kindling a fire to offer his son as a burnt offering to God. To say it another way, it meant putting on the altar all his hopes, dreams, aspirations, and affections. It meant dying to the son of his love. It meant giving God *his best*. His everything.

Abraham didn't understand. Why was God asking him to kill his son? To murder his own son seemed contrary to everything God represented. But he decided to obey God's voice. His obedience to the voice of God brought him through to God's intended end. Worship, therefore, is giving God everything in obedience to His voice.

LEARNING TO LOVE

To love others well is a skill we intentionally develop. We're not born good lovers. Paul taught on love's true essence in 1 Corinthians 13 because he recognized it's something we need to learn and grow in. First we learn what it is, then we mature in expressing it.

Worship is an expression of love. Therefore, worship is learned. The ability to worship is not a talent we're born with.

Rather, it's a grace we develop and grow in. All of us devote ourselves, therefore, to constantly developing and deepening the way we express our worship to God. We may read books and receive instruction on how to worship, but at the end of the day, we learn to worship by doing it.

Don't be impatient with yourself if you don't know how to worship as you desire. Just keep growing. The Holy Spirit will teach you when you don't know how to pray as you ought (Rom 8:26). Learning to worship is not a goal to attain but a journey to walk. We never stop learning how to give Him more of our hearts.

In our churches, we've been taught to work, and taught to witness. But have we been taught to worship?

Worship is described passionately in Psalm 42:7, "Deep calls unto deep at the roar of Your waterfalls." Overwhelming circumstances often open the deepest places of our hearts. Worship is the deep within us calling out to the deep in God.

Sometimes worship goes beyond words. Love does not need to be verbalized in order to be expressed. Sometimes more is said simply through eye contact than could ever be expressed verbally. Worship involves "eye contact" with God. Worship is staring at God.

One of the best ways to learn about worship is to observe the worship of heaven in the book of Revelation. It will be a glorious day when we're gathered around the throne of God, free from all hindrances and shackles of self-consciousness, and liberated to worship Him with our entire beings! But get this—we don't have to wait for heaven; we can worship Him now just like we will in glory. Heaven is noisy and passionate in its demonstration of praise and worship to God. God loves passionate expressions of worship because He Himself is fiercely passionate. We will never go wrong in using the heavenly prototype of worship as a pattern today. As we gain insight into heaven's worship, we can then pray that we experience worship "on earth as it is in heaven" (Matt 6:10).

We learn from heaven's example to be *spontaneous* in worship. True love in marriage sometimes has a mundane element to it, but the spark of romance is rekindled through spontaneity. An unplanned gift or excursion or restaurant stop can add spice to true love. Similarly, spontaneous expressions of worship can strengthen our intimacy with Jesus. Respond to the small impulses and discover new ways of expressing love to God.

Worship is *response*. The Lord initiates His love toward us, and we respond by loving in return. It takes God to love God. What I mean is, the love He pours into our hearts empowers us to love Him back. We can't love Him properly until we first receive His love. One of the greatest roles of the Holy Spirit in our lives is to empower us to love Jesus with the same love the Father has for Jesus (John 17:26). When He empowers us to worship in this manner, our hearts come alive!

THE HOLY SPIRIT AND WORSHIP

We can experience the intimacy and flow of worship only as the Holy Spirit indwells us and empowers us. To worship, we're totally dependent on the Spirit.

Paul described the circle of worship when he wrote, "For of Him and through Him and to Him are all things, to whom be glory forever" (Rom 11:36). First of all, worship is *of Him*. He created, designed, and initiated it. Then it is *through Him*—that is, it happens only through His enabling power. Then it is *to Him*, in that all worship is lifted up to Him who sits on the throne. So it starts with Him and, coming full circle, ends with Him.

In corporate worship gatherings, the Holy Spirit is our Worship Leader. The role of *a worship leader* is to follow the promptings of *The Worship Leader*. Every corporate worship service is a glorious adventure of following the impulses of the Holy Spirit. It's fitting for worship leaders to bring a list of songs to a meeting, but a meeting is not successful if we've merely followed our list; it's successful if we've followed the Spirit.

Worship leaders follow the Holy Spirit in a manner that is somewhat similar to the way the Israelites followed the cloud of God's glory in the wilderness (Num 9:15-23). When the cloud moved, they moved; when the cloud stayed, they pitched their tents and stayed. With every song we sing, worship leaders are seeking to discern how long the Spirit is resting on that song, and they don't want to move from it until "the cloud moves forward." If the Spirit of God hasn't moved on yet from where we are in this moment, why should we? Following the cues of the Spirit is much more refreshing than following the cues of our service order. Not only does the Holy Spirit want to lead our times of corporate worship, He's really good at it.

God has promised, "I will instruct you and teach you in the way you should go; I will guide you with My eye. Do not be like the horse or like the mule, which have no understanding, which must be harnessed with bit and bridle, else they will not come near you" (Ps 32:8-9). I'd like to apply these verses to the way the Holy Spirit wants to lead us in the way we should go in worship. Mules have a way of dragging and falling behind; horses have a way of charging and getting ahead of things. The Holy Spirit wants us to do neither, but to draw close and stay in step with Him. To follow the subtle inclinations of the Holy Spirit in worship, we must be continually sensitive to His voice.

WORSHIP IN SPIRIT AND TRUTH

Jesus divulged the greatest revelation on worship to a foreigner—a Samaritan woman—when He said, "God is Spirit, and those who worship Him must worship in spirit and truth" (John 4:24). Let me remind you about the context of that statement.

Jesus had come to the town of Sychar, and He rested at the well on the town's outskirts while the disciples went off to buy food. A Samaritan woman from town came to draw water at the well, and Jesus asked her for a drink. In the course of the conversation, He revealed that He had divine knowledge about her life. She realized she was in the presence of a prophet, so she came out with the nagging question of her soul: "Our fathers worshiped on this mountain, and you Jews say that in Jerusalem is the place where one ought to worship" (John 4:20). Here's what was behind her question.

The Jews believed that Jerusalem was the place God had chosen to meet with His people, but the Samaritans used Deuteronomy 11:29 to convince themselves Mount Gerizim was the right place. Torn by the theological arguments and desperate to encounter God, what she was really asking was, "What's the right place to connect with God?" She wanted to worship and know God.

She was articulating the global cry of the human heart. People everywhere have a deep longing to connect with God. This is why seekers visit our churches. Even if they can't articulate it clearly, their hearts are reaching to connect with God. This is why the Lord's house is first and foremost a house of prayer (Isa 56:7). It's a place where people can come and connect with God. If the meeting never becomes a prayer meeting, people may leave having connected with *us* but they will have missed the whole point—connecting with *God*.

The best way a worship team can help people connect with God is by connecting with God themselves. When observers see that the team's connection with God is real, they'll find courage to join in and worship.

When Jesus looked at this woman, He knew she was a sinner. But that didn't distract Him. Because sin doesn't trip God up. He knows we're sinners. Jesus looked past her sins and saw a yearning, hungry heart. And He answered her question with some great news. "You're wanting to connect with God? I have good news for you. He's eagerly desiring to connect with you!"

Well, here's literally how He said it:

> "Woman, believe Me, the hour is coming when you will neither on this mountain, nor in Jerusalem, worship the Father. You worship what you do not know; we know what we worship, for salvation is of the Jews. But the hour is coming, and now is, when the

true worshipers will worship the Father in spirit and truth; for the Father is seeking such to worship Him. God is Spirit, and those who worship Him must worship in spirit and truth" (John 4:21-24).

The good news was that the Father is a Seeker. He is fervently seeking to connect with people. We are *the yearning of His heart* (Isa 63:15). Jesus didn't say the Father is seeking worship, but worshipers. He's not seeking outward forms of worship, but inner sincerity and wholehearted affection. He wants the heart—all of it.

Jesus said we worship the Father *in spirit and truth*. Let's examine what is means to *worship in spirit*, and then to *worship in truth*.

WORSHIP IN SPIRIT

By saying we worship the Father *in spirit*, the first thing Jesus meant was that worship is no longer confined to one geographical location. To her question regarding Jerusalem versus Mount Gerizim as the designated place of worship, Jesus was basically saying, "Neither. The way to connect with God will no longer be at one specific mountain." Jesus knew the time was shortly to come when Mosaic sacrifices at Jerusalem would be outdated, and worship would occur within the New Testament temple—the hearts of people (1 Cor 3:16). Believers now worship the Father at any time and at any place in the world. This is fabulous!

Secondly, *worship in spirit* meant that worship is no longer a function of rites and ceremonies but proceeds directly from the human spirit. Under the old covenant, worship was a series of outward ceremonies that did not necessarily involve the heart of the participants. Through Isaiah, God lamented, "These people draw near with their mouths and honor Me with their lips, but have removed their hearts far from Me, and their fear toward Me is taught by the commandment of men" (Isa 29:13). Jesus inaugurated a new and better covenant in which worship is not merely the mouthing of empty clichés but rather the sincere expression of a pure heart. God no longer wants ceremonial worship at a fixed locality; He now desires worshipers who will worship in purity of spirit. He wants worship that is genuine, real, and heartfelt.

Thirdly, by saying we *worship in spirit*, Jesus meant we worship through the agency of the *Holy Spirit*. Paul confirmed we "worship God in the Spirit" (Phil 3:3). Jesus gave us the Holy Spirit so that we might be released and enabled to worship. When we worship, we literally soar in the Spirit. Lifted on the winds of the Spirit, we are caught up in the beauty and brilliance of Jesus Christ. Worship in the Spirit is so sublime that it's actually pleasurable (Ps 16:11). The heights to be explored in worship are so lofty that they expand above us as a veritable universe for our exploration.

WORSHIP IN TRUTH

And now, what does it mean to *worship in truth*? For starters, it means that we worship with our mind. In our John 4 passage above, Jesus distinguished between *ignorant* worship ("you worship what you do not know"), and *intelligent* worship ("we know what we worship"). Worship that involves only the spirit is insufficient; for worship to be intelligent, it must include the mind. In other words, worship is not only a floating, ethereal feeling that sweeps us up into a state of existential harmony with the universe; rather, it's something that involves the entirety of our cerebral faculties. True worship is experienced at the height of mental awareness. The more we focus our minds on the object of our worship—the Lord Jesus—the more meaningful our worship becomes. Some people have lamented that the lyrics of certain songs require too much mental concentration. Perhaps they've missed the whole point that worship is *supposed* to be mentally engaging.

The second obvious implication of *worship in truth* is that worship must happen through Jesus Christ, who is the truth (John 14:6). We worship through the mediation of our great High Priest, through whom we approach God. And the object of our worship is Christ Himself.

Thirdly, *worship in truth* means we worship in *authentici-ty*. The opposite of authentic worship is hypocritical worship. We have an example of hypocritical worship in the life of King Saul.

After defeating the Amalekites, Saul wanted Samuel to offer a burnt offering to the Lord so they could worship to-gether in the presence of the people. But Samuel was dis-pleased with Saul because of his disobedience and didn't want to stay. Samuel told Saul that God had rejected him as king. Nevertheless, Saul still wanted Samuel to stay and officiate a sacrifice so that he could be honored before the elders and the people. Reluctantly, Samuel went back with Saul, offered the sacrifice, and "Saul worshiped the Lord" (1 Sam 15:31). It was not true worship, however, but a pretense for the sake of Saul's insecure ego. Saul wasn't interested in worshiping the Lord; he was interested in saving face before the people. He wanted the people to think he had Samuel's and God's favor.

Before we criticize Saul too severely, let's consider wheth-er we've ever been tempted to worship for hypocritical rea-sons. For example, have you ever had a time when you were living in compromise and really not right in your heart to-ward God, but you pretended to worship because you didn't want the people next to you to discern your lukewarm con-dition? Or has there been a moment when, realizing that oth-ers were watching you, you suddenly made yourself appear more engaged in worship than you really were? God is not interested in worship that wants to look good in front of oth-er people. He wants worship that comes from a heart that is pure and *true*.

To explain my meaning, let me clarify that God wants us to come before Him even when there's something between us. If you're not right with God, just be honest about it. Draw near, and tell Him how pained you are over your sin. Be open about it with Him. To *worship in truth* doesn't mean we must be perfect; it just means we're not hiding anything or mak-ing pretenses. It's not hypocritical to praise the Lord despite negative feelings or known sin as long as we're willing to acknowledge those issues. We expose those things to His light. In contrast, hypocritical worship attempts to cover the inner issues by putting on a spiritual front, all the while denying the Holy Spirit access to the recesses of our hearts. Let's resolve to worship Him in *authenticity*.

Finally, *worship in truth* means that we worship God through the truth of His word, for *His word is truth* (John 17:17). This means we use biblical language as we express our love for Jesus. If we worship God in sincerity but not according to the truth of His word, our worship is false. For example, millions of sincere people worship Allah, the god of Islam, but it isn't true worship because God didn't reveal Himself in Scripture as the Allah of Mohammed. He is the God and Father of our Lord Jesus Christ (Rom 15:6). Sincerity in worship is not enough; to sincerity we must add truth.

One marvelous way to worship in truth is to worship with the Scriptures open before you. As you read a verse, take time to worship the Lord according to the content of that verse, speaking the language of the verse back to God. Of the 31,103 verses in the Bible, many are tremendous fuel for igniting worship.

When you worship in the truth of God's word, the word becomes flesh—in you. Truth moves from your head down to your heart. Every atom of your being begins to align with truth. Holiness becomes more than a doctrine but a way of life. Christology is not just correct doctrine about Christ in your head, but Christ begins to stand upright inside you and express Himself through you. Love becomes more than just a virtue you understand, but it begins to permeate through every pore of your being. When you worship in truth, truth becomes incarnate *in you*.

DAVID WORSHIPED IN TRUTH

David was a "word guy." What I mean is, he worshiped with the Scriptures in front of him. He had a remarkable practice: He would grab his guitar (harp), sit before the ark of the covenant, gaze upon the glory of God, open the Torah (Moses' law was his Bible), focus on a Scripture, begin to strum the guitar, and then the song would start. As he sang the Scriptures, torrents of love would begin to flow and he would be caught up in the Spirit.

This was where David's *sweet psalmist anointing* originated (2 Sam 23:1). The psalmist anointing wasn't primarily a platform anointing but a secret place anointing. The songs were birthed in the secret place and from there went viral.

I have a theory I can't prove with a verse, but I think David's favorite book was Deuteronomy. Here's why. When you find a word in Deuteronomy and then flip over to David's psalms, you find that word everywhere. In Deuteronomy, the Lord is called a refuge. Go to David's psalms and it's refuge, refuge, refuge. In Deuteronomy, the Lord is a shield. Go to David's psalms and it's shield, shield, shield. In Deuteronomy, the Lord is a King. Go to David's psalms and it's King, King, King. In Deuteronomy, the Lord is a rock. Go to David's psalms and it's rock, rock, rock.

"David, what are you doing?"

I'll tell you what he's doing. He's sitting before the ark with the guitar in hand, taking a Scripture and going deep in it. "You're my Rock. You're my Rock. Immovable. Unshakable. My immunity from the breakers of the sea. My security in the windy storm. My sure foundation. When the floods come, my house will not be swept away. When everything else changes, You remain unchanging. You're my Rock."

As he worshiped from a verse, his spirit soared in the Holy Spirit, and the psalms were born.

Someone said, "They're having a night of worship at our church, so I guess I don't need to take my Bible with me." Pardon me, but your Bible contains 31,103 verses to empower your worship—and you're going to go to a night of worship without it? May we be so awakened to the glory of God's word, and the marvelous way it aids our worship, that we take it to every worship context we ever attend. May we discover David's secret of using the word as a catalyst for worship.

KITE METAPHOR

When I think of *worship in spirit and truth*, I find the metaphor of a kite helpful. A kite wants to harness the power of the wind and soar into the skies. It eagerly strains toward the highest heights. That's worship in spirit. When you enter into worship, your spirit wants to soar ever higher in the glorious adventure of experiencing and expressing the love of Christ. Your spirit seems to recognize there's a heavenly firmament to explore in the majestic love of Christ. I'm calling that *worship in spirit*.

As a kite is straining for the skies, if you decide your string is too short and you let go the string because you think the kite deserves to soar higher than your string allows, guess what happens next. The kite collapses and flaps to the ground. Why? Because it had to be grounded by the string if it was to soar in the heavens.

The grounding of the kite to the earth represents *worship in truth*. For your heart to soar in worship, it must be grounded in truth. It's your foundations in truth that enable your spirit to soar in worship. Truth represents a firmament below you that you can explore all your days; and spirit represents a firmament above you that you can explore all your days. Worship is the glorious exploration of both universes. How deep can you go in truth, and how high can go in the Spirit?

There's a trend in the church today that I find totally delightful: musicians with a Bible open in front of them; singers with a Bible open on their music stand; worship leaders leading with the Scriptures open in front of them. I love it! They're getting it!

The deeper you go in truth, the higher you can soar in the Spirit.

When Jesus said, "the true worshipers will worship the Father in spirit and truth" (John 4:23), He certainly packed a lot into those few choice words! What a simple and yet profound description of worship.

THE SIMPLICITY OF WORSHIP

With so much being written and said about worship today, it can feel like the topic is overwhelming in its immensity and limitless possibilities. In our sincere desire to discover worship's potential, we can find ourselves actually beginning to strain at it. We can become consumed with trying to execute it properly, or trying to exceed the intensity of last week's level. But when we begin to labor and strain at worship, we miss the whole point because worship, in its essence, is profoundly simple.

Not only is it simple, but it's for the simple. It's for those who are childlike enough to give their hearts openly, sincerely, and honestly to the Lord. Worship is not work—it's actually delightful, even fun! Worship is enjoyable and relaxing. Worship should be renewing, invigorating, therapeutic. We must relax if we are to enjoy the simplicity of worship.

When Jesus gave the tremendous revelation in John 4 that we are to worship in spirit and truth, He gave that mighty revelation to a Samaritan woman. And then in Luke 7, the beauty of worship was demonstrated by a known sinner who anointed the feet of Jesus when He was in her hometown. The fact that the Holy Spirit chose two ordinary women to illustrate worship's beauty demonstrates that worship is not intricate or complicated but simple and within reach of all. Worship is simply opening one's heart to God and enjoying a loving, reciprocal relationship with Him.

Worship leaders should be cautious about exerting emotional pressure or coercing people into a more enthusiastic expression of praise or worship. Leaders should invite and inspire but not manipulate. Some leaders have found great effectiveness by relaxing during worship services instead of trying to get the crowd "worked up." It's understandable for worship leaders to want the people to participate enthusiastically, and everyone loves it when a service roars and soars into "the high praises of God" (Ps 149:6). But rather than pressuring people toward high praise, let's rely on the Holy Spirit to empower and lead it.

Some of the most beautiful times in worship are when it's expressed in simplicity and serenity. We may as well relax, delight in being with God, and enjoy the degree of glory which the Holy Spirit chooses to give. Rather than continually straining for some euphoric *high*, let's enjoy the simplicity of worship.

Worship leaders, does it take a great spiritual experience on the heights of Zion to make us happy with a given worship service? If we derive our fulfillment from the intensity of each worship service, we are sure to be frustrated. If worship must attain a certain intensity in order for us to be at peace with ourselves, then everything we do is tainted with fleshly energy, concern, and effort. If the service doesn't take off according to our expectations, increased levels of exertion can turn into hype. Let's find our joy and peace in something other than the intensity of praise and worship attained in a service. May our peace be drawn from Christ and our abiding relationship with Him, not from the relative success of a worship service. May we find contentment in a *simple* expression of worship and rest on the unmoving Rock, Christ Jesus.

THE FIRST COMMANDMENT IN FIRST PLACE

Although this book is directed primarily to congregational worship, worship relates to all of life. Our love for the Lord is expressed in and through all we do. Jesus wants our love relationship with Him to be the first priority of each day.

Jesus was once asked, "Teacher, which is the great commandment in the law?" Jesus answered, "You shall love the Lord your God with all your heart, with all your soul, and with all your mind." Then He added this perspective: "This is the first and great commandment. And the second is like it: 'You shall love your neighbor as yourself'" (Matt 22:38-39). Jesus called love for God the *first commandment* and love for neighbor the *second commandment*.

Jesus wants our love for Him to be first in our lives. Worshiping Him is our first priority, even more important than serving others. Love for neighbor comes in at a very close second, but it's still second. Nothing must be allowed to usurp or supplant love for God as the first and greatest thing in our lives.

Keep first things first. When our love for God gets our first and best attention, then we will function in the spiritual wholeness necessary to execute the second commandment. When our priorities become inverted and we begin placing more emphasis on loving others than loving God, we are headed for burnout. The only way to remain fervent and wholehearted is to keep returning to our first love (Rev 2:4).

The Holy Spirit is profoundly committed to keeping the first commandment in first place in our lives. When we are standing before God in worship, we find our true identity. *I'm not primarily a worker for God; I'm first and foremost a lover of God.* Worship establishes us in our true identity before the throne. We're not primarily a labor force for Jesus, we're a bride. For some, the Holy Spirit is visiting us and turning upside down the tables of our priorities. He wants us established in our primary identity as lovers of God. By the time He's finished in our lives, we'll be lovers who work rather than workers who love.

I know from experience what it's like to get the second commandment in first place. When the Lord corrected me, He said, "Bob, you come to Me like a gas station." Now, I consider a gas station to be a necessary evil. I don't like to fill up with gas; I like to drive. But I know that in order to drive, I must first fill up with gas. The Lord was saying, "Bob, you worship Me in order to get filled up. You don't come to Me because I'm the first love of your heart; you come to Me to get recharged so you can pursue the first love of your life." You see, my first love was the ministry. I loved to drive! I wanted to see souls saved; I wanted to win my city for Christ; I wanted to change the world. I was motivated more by what I did for God than by being with Him. I claimed, "All my springs are in You" (Psalm 87:7), but in fact what sustained me most was the satisfaction of ministry accomplishments. The Lord helped me see that the second commandment had found first place in my heart.

This was a very painful realization for me. I fell before Him and cried, "Lord, I'm sorry; this isn't how I want it to be. I don't want to have a filling station relationship with You. I want it to be about love. I want You to be the great love of my life."

I sensed the Lord responding, "Yes, son, I know that's what you want. And that's why I'm revealing your heart. I've come to allure you into the wilderness (Hos 2:14), and there I will awaken you to a depth of love relationship beyond what you've known."

To align my heart, the Lord simply removed my ministry. It was agonizing. I cried, "Lord, why does this hurt so much? You haven't removed Your presence from my life; all You've done is remove my ministry. Should it hurt this much?" I began to see how serving God had become the fountain of my soul. He was inviting me to return to the simplicity of delighting in just being with Him.

I was being restored in adoration and worship.

He wanted me addicted to the wine of His love (Song 1:2), instead of the wine of ministry. Ministry can be intoxicating. When God uses you to strengthen His bride, it can give you a buzz. Her face lights up with the glory of God, and you feel the reward of watching God honor your obedience and labor. But the wine of ministry doesn't strengthen your devotion for Christ, it goes to your head and distorts your thinking. It can make you feel strong, powerful, invincible.

So the Lord comes to us, like He did to the Ephesians who were so successful in ministry, and He says, "I'm calling you back to your first love" (Rev 2:4). He wants us to be people of one thing—the passionate pursuit of His face.

David said, "One thing I have desired of the Lord, that will I seek: that I may dwell in the house of the Lord, and to inquire in His temple" (Ps 27:4). David chased after *one thing*—the face of God. Paul said, "But one thing I do"—which was the pursuit of "the upward call of God in Christ Jesus" (Phil 3:13-14); Mary of Bethany discovered that "one thing is needed," and Jesus added that she had "chosen that good part, which will not be taken away from her" (Luke 10:42). There's only one thing that's really necessary, and that is to sit lovingly at Jesus' feet and hear His words. It's the first commandment in first place, the pursuit of a loving relationship with our dazzling Bridegroom.

Someone may be concerned that too much emphasis on worship can turn the church into an ingrown "bless-me club," as though an emphasis on worship would cause the church to neglect evangelistic outreach. Nothing should be further from the truth. True worship should awaken us to the ripe harvest all around us. Worship expands our perspective, moves our focus from ourselves to God, and catches His passion for the lost. True worshipers carry a zeal for the harvest—motivated by a fiery affection for the face of Jesus.

CHAPTER 5

BECOMING A WORSHIPER

Jesus told us the Father is seeking worshipers (John 4:23). Why? Because He loves both the heart and sacrifices of worshipers. Their lifestyles arise as a fragrant aroma before Him. This is why believers are on a quiet, inner quest to be true worshipers. We want to touch and move the heart of God.

What does it mean to become a worshiper? Someone in the Bible whose example has inspired me personally is that of the sinful woman in Luke 7:36-50 who anointed Jesus' feet. Look at the story again, and let's consider how this woman demonstrated the heart of a true worshiper.

Then one of the Pharisees asked Him to eat with him. And He went to the Pharisee's house, and sat down to eat. And behold, a woman in the city who was a sinner, when she knew that Jesus sat at the table in the Pharisee's house, brought an alabaster flask of fragrant oil, and stood at His feet behind Him weeping; and she began to wash His feet with her tears, and wiped them with the hair of her head; and she kissed His feet and anointed them with the fragrant oil.

Now when the Pharisee who had invited Him saw this, he spoke to himself, saying, "This Man, if He were a prophet, would know who and what manner of woman this is who is touching Him, for she is a sinner."

And Jesus answered and said to him, "Simon, I have something to say to you."

So he said, "Teacher, say it."

"There was a certain creditor who had two debtors. One owed five hundred denarii, and the other fifty. And when they had nothing with which to repay, he freely forgave them both. Tell Me, therefore, which of them will love him more?"

Simon answered and said, "I suppose the one whom he forgave more."

And He said to him, "You have rightly judged."

Then He turned to the woman and said to Simon, "Do you see this woman? I entered your house; you gave Me no water for My feet, but she has washed My feet with her tears and wiped them with the hair of her head. You gave Me no kiss, but this woman has not ceased to kiss My feet since the time I came in. You did not anoint My head with oil, but this woman has anointed My feet with fragrant oil. Therefore I say to you, her sins, which are many, are forgiven, for she loved much. But to whom little is forgiven, the same loves little."

Then He said to her, "Your sins are forgiven."

And those who sat at the table with Him began to say

to themselves, "Who is this who even forgives sins?"
Then He said to the woman, "Your faith has saved
you. Go in peace."

WORSHIPERS ARE GIVERS

Using this woman as an example of a worshiper, let's look
at some qualities of worshipers. The first lesson I see in her
extravagance is that worshipers are givers.

This woman poured valuable perfume on Jesus. We don't
know how valuable this oil might have been. The "very costly oil of spikenard" that Mary poured upon Jesus in Bethany
was valued at roughly a year's wages (Mark 14:3-5). That was
a different incident. Was the fragrant oil of this sinful woman
of equal value? It's unclear. If it was, it could have represented her life savings. What *does* seem clear is that this fragrant
oil was more valuable than simply a flask of olive oil. By pouring this oil on Jesus, she was making a significant sacrifice.

This flask of oil was probably not like our jars of perfume
today. Our perfume bottles have spray pumps that dispense
only a little liquid at a time; or we can unscrew the bottle lid
and dab a little perfume here and there. But this woman's jar
or flask was likely made of ceramic or pottery. It didn't have
a screw cap, so the most likely way to get to the contents
was to break the jar. Once broken, all the jar's contents would
probably need to be used at once. In bringing this perfume
to Jesus, she realized there was no way to give only part; it
was all or nothing. This made her offering extravagant, even
wasteful. But she gave without hesitation over the cost. In
fact, the cost made it all the sweeter for her. Love carried her
heart in this beautiful expression of lavish affection.

To some observers, lavish expressions of worship can appear wasteful. But in one sense, there's something wasteful
about all our lives. All of us have a choice—will we waste our
lives on ourselves or Jesus?

The Scriptures encourage us to bring a gift when coming
to worship the Lord. Psalm 96:8-9 exhorts, "Bring an offering,
and come into His courts. Oh, worship the Lord in the beauty

of holiness!" In the Old Testament sacrificial system, worshipers were obligated to bring an animal sacrifice (such as a lamb, goat, ram, or turtledove). They were not to appear before God without a gift. "None shall appear before Me empty-handed" (Exod 23:15). Worshipers will prepare an offering when they come to a worship service because worship is always wanting to give. I once heard Jack Hayford say he never would allow an offering plate to go past him without putting something into it. Inspired by his example, I've always tried to be ready to give *something* when I'm in a meeting where an offering is received. The amount is not always the significant thing but the desire to participate in the corporate exercise of bringing an offering.

When we become abandoned worshipers, tithing ceases to be a difficult practice. It's our joy. And offerings beyond the tithe become a delightful privilege. Because worshipers are givers.

Giving financially to the kingdom of God is an integral part of our worship. The way some church liturgies have developed, the offering time sometimes feels disconnected from the worship service. In some churches, we worship, then we listen to the week's announcements, then we have the offering, and then the sermon. To separate giving from the worship service is, in my opinion, unfortunate. The dignity and honor of giving to the Lord from the strength of our labors should be intentionally designed as an integral part of worship. I suggest, therefore, that church leaders look for ways to make the giving of tithes and offerings a vital part of our worship services.

One way to help our giving be more heartfelt is to do it differently from time to time. Do ushers usually pass a plate? Then invite the believers to carry their offering to the front some Sunday. Do people usually give at offering boxes placed at the back of the sanctuary? Then do something different sometime, and receive the offering in a different way. For example, in the course of the singing, families could be invited to come forward together, even kneel together, and place their offerings on the altar. Different approaches can bump us out of our routines and renew our authenticity in giving.

Let me throw out another creative way to make giving a stronger act of worship. Encourage the church family, perhaps on a specific Sunday, to bring their offering to church in the form of cash. Greenbacks. Currency. Because something happens inside when we give actual cash. Maybe it's just psychological, but when we give real money, it can feel like the gift is more real. When we fill out a check or give electronically, it doesn't feel so hard. For some reason, it feels easier to charge $100 on a credit card than to dole out five $20 bills. (Credit card companies are very aware of this and always push credit card sales over cash.) Giving cash seems to engage the heart more. Understanding this dynamic, you could plan a service in which worshipers are invited to offer their cash in a specific way in worship.

Whether or not that's a good idea, my point is this: Let's look for ways to make giving in our corporate gatherings a heartfelt expression of worship to the Lord.

WORSHIPERS ARE PASSIONATE

When this woman came into Jesus' presence, she was weeping. Whatever was going on in her heart, she was feeling it deeply. The tears and poured oil reflected her wholehearted repentance, affection, and gratefulness. Movie actors or actresses may know how to weep on the set when the cameras are recording, but this woman's tears weren't contrived. They revealed a sincere, unveiled heart.

When I wrote the first edition of this book in 1986, I wrote the following: "I will confess that as a man I find it very difficult to cry. Few are the times when I come to tears before God. And that concerns me, because I ask, 'Lord, is my heart too hard before you? I want to be soft and tender in Your presence!' The times of worship that have been most meaningful to me are the times when I cried before God. Brokenness and tears are truly key elements in worship."

Now, over thirty years later, I'm a profoundly different person. The Lord has used the crushing circumstances of life to break the strength of my youth, and in the process has made me a weeper. I realize He answered the cry I articulated in this book over thirty years ago. More than ever, I appreciate the beauty and significance of tears in worship. Never relent until you weep while meditating in the word of God. Be satisfied only with a soft, tender heart that is moved deeply with longing for the fullness of Christ.

We see also that this woman kissed Jesus' feet. This is an authentic way to express worship, for the Greek word for worship—*proskuneo*—means *to kiss the hand toward; to do reverence or homage by kissing the hand; to bow one's self in adoration*. The derivation of *proskuneo* is thought to come from the Greek word for dog. Thus, the original meaning was *to kiss, like a dog licking his master's hand*. When I first discovered this, I was somewhat repulsed by the idea. I asked, "Lord, am I like a dog before You? Is that all I mean to You?" But then the Lord began to highlight some beautiful lessons through the etymology of this word.

Although I have always been a dog lover, I owned a dog for only a few years while growing up. Among my fondest memories of *Buster* are the times when we would come home and be greeted by him at the door. From outside, we could hear his tail thumping against the wall and his paws scratching at the door. And when we stepped inside, he was all over us! Jumping, licking, wagging, thumping, twirling— you would have thought he hadn't seen us for weeks! As I remembered those royal welcomes, the Lord whispered to my heart, "How excited are you about being with Me again, when you enter My house?" I realized, then, that this aspect of a dog's nature should mark true worshipers.

Anyone who has ever had a dog knows what it's like to be sitting, perhaps reading, and look over to see the dog just lying there staring. "What are you looking at, mutt?" He seems to talk back with his eyes, "Silly, you know what I want." Finally, tired of being scrutinized, the dog's master asks, "Do you want to go outside?" Thump, thump, thump. That is what he was waiting for!

Similarly for us, there is an element of waiting in worship—simply staring at the Lord. Worship isn't incessant chatter. Sometimes it's quietly resting in His presence, waiting to hear His voice. When you have a close relationship with someone, communication can sometimes happen without words. Sometimes a look can say things that words can't. Take the time to behold the Lord. Then, when He stirs, we're aware of it.

Then there's the time when the dog comes over to sit by the chair. But he isn't satisfied with sitting next to his master; he has to plop his body right on top of his master's feet. Dogs desire the closeness of physical contact. We desire the same kind of nearness with our Lord. We want to draw close to His heart in worship and lean upon His breast.

WORSHIPERS ARE UNASHAMED

This woman was so taken with Jesus that she wouldn't allow the perceptions of others to deter her. She gave herself in worship to the Lord, realizing that others might even misunderstand her courage and devotion.

Since Luke described this woman as *sinful*, some have supposed she was a prostitute. When she washed Jesus' feet, she let down her hair—a common act for a prostitute in that day. The disciples were no doubt wondering what was going to happen next. Was she coming on to Jesus? When she first entered the room, everyone pretended not to notice. But when she let down her hair, all eyes must have nervously glanced her way.

Worshipers can't go unnoticed. Their extravagance attracts attention. This is one reason some are overly restrained in worship—afraid of what others might think of them if they really show their feelings for Jesus. Peer pressure can have a positive—but also negative—effect on worship. It's kept many from the blessing of opening their hearts to the Lord. Some folks might say, "Oh, that's just Joanie doing her thing again." Others might shake their heads and think, "Straaaange." But reproach is sometimes part of the cost of being a true worshiper.

Obviously this woman was not following the conventional forms of worship. There's no mention in Psalms of pouring perfume on our Lord's feet. Weeping and kissing and hair—David didn't really give us any instruction concerning these things. Just because an expression of worship appears unique or excessive doesn't mean it's invalid or out of order. When the feelings of the heart are expressed, love is not bound by protocol or rules.

She had tried to fill her longing for love in men, but now she had found the Lover of her soul. So why not give her love to Him unabashedly? Worship gravitates toward the extravagant.

Another insight into worship can be seen in Simon's derogatory thought: "This Man, if He were a prophet, would know who and what manner of woman this is who is touching Him, for she is a sinner" (Luke 7:39). Worshipers are sometimes controversial. Some might be affirming, but others are critical.

David was reproached by Michal, for example, when he danced before the ark of the Lord with all his might. Michal was King Saul's daughter, and she despised the thought that a king would behave in such an undignified manner in the presence of the nation. So she scoffed, "How glorious was the king of Israel today, uncovering himself today in the eyes of the maids of his servants, as one of the base fellows shamelessly uncovers himself!" (2 Sam 6:20). Michal paid a price for her cynicism, however. As a result, she was never healed of her barrenness. Her story carries a warning: If we become critical of genuine acts of worship, we could hazard spiritual barrenness.

Something inside shrivels when we despise another worshiper.

But worship is controversial. Everyone seems to have their own musical and stylistic preferences. Churches have split over worship styles and preferences. Congregations have fallen to spiritual barrenness because they resisted authentic expressions of true worship.

The sinful woman in our passage didn't seem to be pleasing any of the people around her, but her sacrifice was pleasing to Jesus. Sometimes we must choose between pleasing man or God. She was willing to endure the censure of others for the sake of giving Jesus her affection.

At first, Jesus seemed to ignore this woman. Her presence was so obvious that everyone was a little nervous, waiting to see what Jesus would do in response. I wonder what the disciples were thinking. *Why is Jesus acting like He doesn't see her? Why doesn't He do something? This woman is obviously out of order. Why doesn't He rebuke her? Why is He letting this thing drag on?* Eventually, Luke tells us that Jesus turned to the woman. The disciples probably sighed in relief. *Finally! Finally Jesus is going to bring correction to this situation.* But instead of rebuking her, Jesus affirmed her. Everyone was probably stunned. But when you stop to think about it, it's comforting to realize how Jesus responded to her heartfelt worship. He accepted her just for who she was, and He'll do the same with us. Although others might be skeptical, He's eager to receive our sincere love and devotion.

Jesus never despises wholehearted affection.

WORSHIPERS ARE CHILDLIKE

As a Pharisee, Simon would have been schooled in worship. He would have studied David, the Psalms, and the Hebrews' long history of worship. His mastery of this topic would have far surpassed that of the sinful woman. In fact, if you were hosting a worship workshop, you might want someone like Simon to teach the session. He had a coherent, orthodox, clear theology of worship. He may have even written manuscripts on the topic. But when it came to actually honoring the Lord, his heart was distant and disengaged. A sinful woman who knew practically nothing about how to exegete biblical texts on worship demonstrated true worship, because of a grateful heart, in the presence of this dignified Pharisee.

Worship is more than a theology; it's an effusion of affection.

This woman's simplicity and childlikeness schooled not only the Pharisee, but also the disciples. The disciples sat at Jesus' feet, so they probably had considerable knowledge about worship. But it took a sinful woman—someone who was uneducated about worship—to model worship for the disciples.

The longer we're with Jesus, and the more we mature in our faith, the more we're inclined to be like the disciples—stodgy, staid, and stuffy in worship. Do we somehow think we outgrow worship? Is it normal to expect that, the longer we're in the faith, the more reserved our worship will become? I think the answer's *no*.

Even elders are childlike. The more we get to know Jesus, the more heartfelt and extravagant our worship becomes. Worship is the domain of elders. Psalm 107:32 says, "Let them...praise Him in the company of the elders." Furthermore, look at the elders in the book of Revelation. They're repeatedly falling prostrate before the throne of God (Rev 4:9-11; 5:8, 14; 11:16; 19:4). The elders around the throne are among the foremost of heaven's examples of worship before the Lamb.

The disciples should have been the examples of a worshiper in this story, but instead they were shown an example. Some of our elders in our churches are still being shown, by the simplest among us, what it means to worship Jesus. As we read these words, let's resolve in our hearts that, as we mature in the knowledge of Christ, we will also grow in our simplicity of worship. The elderly slow down in their bodies but not in their spirits! Even in our elderly years, let's be a worshiper who leads others by example.

May I never become so mature as a believer that I lose my enthusiasm and zeal for the fame of His name!

WORSHIPERS ARE CARRIERS

Worshipers are carriers of the fragrance of Christ. After this anointing, the fragrance that was on Christ was also on this woman. When she left Christ's presence, she continued to carry His fragrance.

The scenario I'm about to depict is not recorded in the Bible, so it probably didn't happen. But my sanctified imagination wonders if something like this could have happened. I imagine Peter, later that day, walking the streets of the city and looking for Jesus. Suddenly, he detects a familiar odor. He recognizes it as the fragrance of the perfume the woman had poured upon Jesus earlier that day. *Jesus must be nearby!* Peter hurries around the corner, expecting to find the Master. But He's not there. Instead, he discovers he's facing the woman who anointed Jesus. It's hours later and she's still carrying the fragrance of Jesus with her.

The same happens with worshipers today. When we give our hearts to the Lord in extravagant worship, we carry with us the aura of Christ. This is the glory of worshipers. We carry the fragrance of Christ everywhere we go (2 Cor 2:14-16). Others recognize we've been with Jesus.

WORSHIP PRECEDED FORGIVENESS

We've seen from this woman's example that worshipers are givers, passionate, unashamed, childlike, and carriers of His presence. Now I want to use her story to show that personal shortcomings are not a hindrance to true worship.

Jesus said to this sinful woman, "Your sins are forgiven." I want to point out He spoke these words *after* she had worshiped. First she worshiped; then she was forgiven. I'm highlighting the sequence. Worship came first; cleansing followed. Jesus didn't require her to get all cleaned up and perfected first before she worshiped. He received her in her current condition.

Jesus still receives us in the same way. We don't have to be perfect before we draw near to Him. Because of the cross, the Father now receives all His children into His presence, even when we're in need of cleansing. The cleansing happens in His presence.

The accuser doesn't want us to believe this. He wants us to think our sins and shortcomings make us unworthy to draw near to God. But his is not the only discouraging voice we hear; we also hear the voice of our conscience. Sometimes our hearts condemn us (1 John 3:20-21). We are experts at self-condemnation. Jesus called us to be perfect like our Father in heaven (Matt 5:48), but we often feel so inadequate. Our conscience beats up on us. The voices of the accuser and our conscience are sometimes very loud, making us tentative and uncertain in our approach to God.

The enemy has one agenda in accusing us: he wants us to feel so unworthy that we avoid God's presence. If he can succeed, sin will find an even stronger foothold in our lives and the darkness in our hearts will deepen.

The sinful woman in our story modeled the way forward. When there's sin in our lives, the answer is found by drawing near to God. We receive the sprinkling of Christ's blood as described in Hebrews 10:22, we draw near in worship and adoration, He forgives and cleanses us, and then His grace empowers us to overcome.

Sometimes we get cleansed first and then worship. And then at other times, like this woman, we worship first and then are cleansed. The sequence is not the point. The point is that we draw near, pour out our affection, receive His cleansing, and live confidently in His embrace. As we worship in intimacy we gain strength to overcome sin. Satan accuses us because He doesn't want us accessing our source of overcoming power.

NO MORE CONDEMNATION

When we seek to draw near to God, sometimes we struggle to distinguish between conviction and condemnation. Let me try to help.

God convicts, but He never condemns. Conviction and condemnation are poles apart. Conviction leads to repentance; condemnation leads to despair. Conviction culminates in victory over sin; condemnation culminates in abject defeat. And here's the biggest difference of all. Conviction draws us toward God; condemnation pulls us away from God. If the impulse you're feeling is making you draw back from God in intimidation, it's condemnation. And God never condemns. Jesus Himself said so: "For God did not send His Son into the world to condemn the world, but that the world through Him might be saved" (John 3:17; see also John 8:11).

There is no condemnation to those who are in Christ Jesus (Rom 8:1). *Condemnation* refers to eternal alienation from God. Before Christ, we were condemned to eternal separation from God. But through faith in Christ (Rom 3:21-22), the condemnation of sin is eternally lifted and we are welcomed into His embrace.

To clarify, Satan still *accuses* us. And the Holy Spirit faithfully *convicts* us. But there's no more *condemnation*. We have been eternally saved from the condemnation of hell.

With the cry of sonship now given to us by the Holy Spirit, we boldly draw near to God. Nothing can stop us from drawing near our Father—not even our own failures, sin, and brokenness. The blood of Jesus on our conscience silences the accuser (Heb 10:22; Rev 12:10-11), and we draw near to worship God in the beauty of holiness.

We don't ever approach God because we feel worthy. Even on our best week, we're still unworthy in ourselves to draw near to God. The only basis for coming close in worship is the blood of Christ and the righteousness of God by faith. We are now children of God! We are now led by the Spirit (Rom 8:14)! And the Spirit leads us boldly right into the throne room of heaven.

If you struggle with a recurring sin, the answer is not in pulling away from God and trying to work it out. The answer is in drawing near and receiving His empowering grace. The glory of His presence affects our sinfulness like radiation affects cancer. As we worship in His presence, the power of sin in our lives is broken and we gain the grace to overcome.

Do you struggle with sin? Then worship! We find this secret in the example of this sinful woman. It's the secret the enemy tries fiercely to hide from us.

Jesus never says to us, "Wait a minute. There's sin in your life. Don't try to get close and love Me in that condition." On the contrary, He says, "Come close. Lean on Me. Let's talk." The only time it's inappropriate to worship God with sin in your life is when you have no intention of changing. But if you're resisting sin and seeking grace to change, draw near with confidence. It's your first step to victory.

God hates our sin. But here's the good news: Sin can't survive in His presence. This is precisely why, when we need cleansing, we must flee into His presence. That's where we receive healing, cleansing, holiness, and purity. This was Charles Wesley's message in these lyrics:

> Jesus, Lover of my soul,
> Let me to Thy bosom fly
> While the nearer waters roll,
> While the tempest still is high!
> Plenteous grace with Thee is found,
> Grace to cover all my sin;
> Let the healing streams abound,
> Make and keep me pure within.

OTHER HINDRANCES TO WORSHIP

It's coming clear. Sin need not hinder us from worshiping because God has made a way. But accusation isn't the only thing that tries to hinder us. Let me list a few other hindrances to worship. My hope is that by shedding light on these hindrances, you'll be enabled to overcome and draw near.

Another deterrent to worship is *pride*. Pride is possibly our greatest hindrance to worship. Pride could have held the sinful woman in our story from worshiping Jesus, but instead she poured herself out for Him. Pride has ruined more worship services than all the forces of hell combined. Pride prefers conservative, low-key, ego-preserving worship. Pride restrains us from lifting our voices in the congregation. Pride robs us of the joy of dancing or lifting our hands or bowing in His presence. Pride incarcerates us in a self-conscious prison of spiritual bondage. Pride says things such as "Well, that's just not my way of praising God."

Worship and pride clash. They can't both flourish at the same time. Worship implicitly kills pride with its self-abasement and humility. Stuffy sophistication has to go. Worship eagerly humbles self so God can be exalted.

David had a unique way of speaking of his glory. For example, he wrote, "I will sing and give praise, even with my glory" (Ps 108:1). By his term *my glory* he meant the reputation and status he had gained as king of Israel. His military conquests made him the greatest world leader of his day. He enjoyed unparalleled prestige, honor, riches, and influence. When it was time to worship, how would the most decorated king on earth conduct himself? He showed us in the above verse. Again, "I will sing and give praise, even with my glory" (Ps 108:1). Here's what he meant.

David would gather his glory—all the splendor of what he had accomplished and accumulated—and pour it all out before the Lord. He went as low as possible. Worship was an opportunity to lift God high by going low. We can do likewise. We can gather all the glory of our attainments, pull ourselves erect to our full height, and then throw it all down prostrate before His glorious majesty. Worshipers love to accrue greater crowns because it gives them even more to cast at His feet. After all, it all came from Him in the first place.

Peer pressure is cousin to pride, and can also hinder our worship. By peer pressure, I mean our natural tendency to be concerned about how we appear in the eyes of others around us. Our flesh wants to look cool and dignified in the eyes of others. The desire for the approval of others can hinder us from giving ourselves wholeheartedly to Jesus in worship. Someone once said, "Never do anything because others are looking at you, and never refrain from anything because others are looking at you."

Presumption is another negative attitude that can hinder worship. We're being presumptuous when we're overly casual with God. "Yo God, whuzzup?" And God might answer, "The voice seems a bit familiar, but I don't recognize the face." Presumption fails to honor God's holiness, and supposes we can approach Him in our own way and on our own terms.

Another hindrance in worship is *spectatorism*. I'm coining that term to refer to the tendency to look around during a worship service, watch everything that's happening, and get so distracted by room dynamics that we never actually worship. While half the room is worshiping, half is watching. Paul made no mention in his epistles, however, of the ministry of surveillance. We're not called to preside but to participate.

Corporate worship too often resembles a spectator sport: The congregation watches while the platform worships. Some worship services would be better described as a worship concert, meaning that there's a ton of energy on the platform while the congregation kicks back and enjoys. But the biblical paradigm for corporate worship was never anything close to a performance/audience model. The Bible calls the whole room a spiritual priesthood (Rom 12:1; 1 Cor 3:16; 1 Pet 2:5-6; Rev 1:6). The purpose of the platform ministry is to unlock and release the praises of the congregation. The worship team is not successful unless they bring the entire congregation with them. We're not spectators but participants in lifting high His glorious praise.

Sentimentalism can also stagnate worship. It's easy to become sentimental over a favorite tune. We've become sentimental in worship when we're more taken with the music than the lyrics. And we've become sentimental in worship when we prefer songs that are familiar over songs that are substantial. Songs that are overly familiar can become sentimental. These songs are so well known that the congregation disengages mentally and simply responds emotionally. The Lord seemed to have this sentimental dynamic in view when He described how Israel was responding to Ezekiel's message. He said to Ezekiel, "Indeed you are to them as a very lovely song of one who has a pleasant voice and can play well on an instrument; for they hear your words, but they do not do them" (Ezek 33:32). God knows how easily we are taken by the beauty of a nice melody without being penetrated by the message. Are we simply grooving to the music without really being gripped by the message of the song?

God made us to delight in music, and there's nothing wrong with enjoying it. But when it comes to worship, music has a holy purpose. God designed music to help us open our hearts and be more responsive to Him. We don't worship music or place our emphasis upon the music itself. Music is a vehicle, not an end in itself. St. Augustine observed, "When I am moved by the voice of him that sings more than by the words sung, I confess to have sinned." We don't want to simply be moved sentimentally by music; we want to be empowered through song to give our hearts in greater ways to God.

Another wrong attitude in worship is *paying lip service.* This happens when we mouth the words of a song but our hearts don't actually own the lyrics. This is halfhearted hypocrisy. We see this same half-heartedness at many times in Israel's history. The Jews would worship heathen gods and then turn around and approach God in worship. (For example, see Ezekiel 14:1-4.) To God, their words were nothing more than lip service. So God responded by saying, "I hate, I despise your feast days, and I do not savor your sacred assemblies. Though you offer Me burnt offerings and your grain offerings, I will not accept them, nor will I regard your fattened peace offerings. Take away from Me the noise of your songs, for I will not hear the melody of your stringed instruments" (Amos 5:21-23). God would rather we keep our mouths shut than worship in pretense.

Something else that hinders some people in corporate worship is being *offended at leadership weaknesses.* For example, someone might think to themselves, "I'm not going to let this worship leader hype me. He can try cheerleading if he wants to, but I'll have no part in it." Just because the worship leader has some weaknesses in his or her style doesn't give me permission to disengage and stage my own private resistance. Even if the worship leader is controlling or self-proclaiming, God is still worthy of my praise.

I'm sure you can identify many more hindrances to worship. Whatever might hinder us, we want to throw off the constraints and give our hearts fully to the Lord Jesus. The sinful woman in the above story didn't allow her sinful past to hinder her from worshiping Jesus. Let's follow her example and renew our resolve to let nothing stop us from abandoning our hearts in adoration for our beloved Lord.

Cast all your crowns!

CHAPTER 6

THE PURPOSE
OF CONGREGATIONAL
WORSHIP

Worship plays a huge role in our corporate gatherings, sometimes involving up to half or more of a meeting's duration. It's essential, therefore, that we have a clear pastoral theology of worship. We want to identify why we worship together, and what we hope to accomplish in our worship services.

Each church must determine for themselves what role they desire worship to fulfill in the life of the local church. Some churches view corporate singing as part of the *preliminaries*, which could be described as those aspects of the service that lead up to the most important element of the service. For some churches, the main event is the preaching of the word; for others, it's the Eucharist. In a preliminaries model, things like singing, announcements, offering, Scripture reading, and special music are viewed as preliminary and preparatory to the main event.

Other churches have a *presence* model of worship. In this model, corporate singing is viewed as a way to encounter the presence of God. On some occasions, presence model churches might tarry in worship longer than anticipated if they sense the presence of God in a particularly strong way. Why? Because they view being in God's presence as not a means to an end (such as preparatory to the sermon), but an end in itself (being with the Lord).

With either model, it's helpful to see corporate worship pointing in three directions. There's a *vertical* aspect to worship, in which our focus is primarily upon the One we love and the One who sits on the throne—the Lord Jesus Christ. Then there's a *horizontal* dynamic to worship, in which we enjoy interpersonal dynamics in the congregation. And finally, worship accomplishes an *inward* work in the heart of each individual worshiper.

I see these three directions of worship reflected in the ministry of the seraphim (also called *living creatures*). Here's how John described them: "The four living creatures, each having six wings, were full of eyes around and within. And they do not rest day or night, saying: 'Holy, holy, holy, Lord God Almighty, who was and is and is to come!'" (Rev 4:8). Their eyes look in three directions simultaneously. Their first preoccupation is with God. They gaze, listen, watch, absorb, search, admire, extol, gape, and thrill at the glory of God. Since eyes usually speak of *intelligence*, we learn from them that the smartest thing we can do is gaze in worship upon the Lord. Secondly, they look around, for it says they "were full of eyes around." As they worship, they look at one another and at all the heavenly host. Thirdly, they look within, for it says they were "full of eyes...within." Part of their gaze in worship is inward.

As we look, therefore, at the way worship looks up, over, and within, we'll gain a stronger understanding of worship's role in the congregation.

VERTICAL DYNAMICS

Let's begin by looking at how worship focuses vertically on the Lord. I'm going to point to just four aspects of going vertical in corporate worship. You can grow your list from here.

1. To bless the Lord

First of all, we worship *to minister to the Lord*. As regards our identity, we are "a royal priesthood" (1 Pet 2:9) and "kings and priests" to God (Rev 1:6). Just as the priests and Levites ministered to the Lord in Moses' tabernacle, believers in the New Covenant are privileged with the same sacred duty. We extol His beauty and goodness, we magnify the greatness of His name, we marvel at His works, and we proclaim the surpassing greatness of His power. In a day when the world blasphemes and curses Him, we lift our hands high and tell Him how excellent He is. We join the angels and living creatures in declaring that He is extravagantly beautiful and altogether lovely.

The cry of the worshiper is not, "Bless me, Lord," but rather, "Bless the Lord, O my soul!" The question is not whether the service blessed us, but whether it blessed Him. The whole thing is for *Him*. And yet, even when we know this, we can be tempted to complain when the worship service doesn't bless us the way we wanted. If someone asks us how the worship service was, we might answer, "Well, on a scale of one to ten, I'd put it right around a five." But if the main purpose for worship is to bless and glorify the Lord, then why am I upset when it doesn't edify me? Who am I to rate the service, anyways? It's *God's* opinion of the worship service that matters. How did it rate on *His* scale? Was *He* pleased with our sacrifice of praise?

Granted, when we bless the Lord, we get blessed in the process. An old Korean quip says, "If you want to smear the face of others with mire, you will have to smear your hands first." And the opposite is equally true: If you bless another then you, too, will be blessed. Proverbs 11:25 says, "He who waters will also be watered himself." By blessing the Lord we're automatically blessed. But we don't bless Him in order to be blessed; we minister to Him without any selfish motive.

We bless Him even if we don't feel blessed in the moment. Why? Because He's worthy of our praise, even if we feel despondent or weary in our souls.

Since worship is all about Jesus, let's be guarded lest we be distracted from looking unto Him. Face it, there are *tons* of potential distractions in congregational worship. We can become so caught up, for example, in asking, "What is God saying today?" that we miss the opportunity simply to love Him. Or we can be derailed by introspection. Sometimes it's appropriate to ask, "Is there any hindering sin in my life?" But sometimes an inward search for sin can actually hinder our calling to minister to the Lord. The blood of Jesus has made us worthy to stand before Him and magnify His name! Searching our hearts for sin is actually the Holy Spirit's job. So if He shows you something for which you need to repent, then do business with God. Otherwise, put yourself aside, lift your face to God, and minister to Him.

The worship service isn't the time for me to get into me; it's time for me to get into God. If we were honest, we'd admit that most of our lives are too self-centered, with everything revolving around personal interests, desires, and concerns. When we're standing before the throne, let's toss all that self-focus. The worship service provides a glorious opportunity to forget about ourselves and get taken up with God.

It's easy, when ministering to the Lord, to get distracted by stuff on the platform. We can become critical of the way the leaders are directing the meeting. Or we can be taken by someone's musicianship or beautiful voice. One time a lady said to me, "Bob, I just love the way you play the piano! I could just sit there for hours and listen to you play." At first, I thought that was a compliment. Later, I realized she was so taken with my piano playing that she had watched, not worshiped. My flourishing musical style had drawn her eyes more to me than to the Lord. I no longer consider it a compliment if my musicianship distracts others from their ministry to the Lord. The purpose of the worship team is to enhance, not divert, the way worshipers engage with the Lord.

Sometimes we catch ourselves thinking along the lines of, "The worship team still hasn't found the flow of the Spirit in this meeting." If we're not careful, we can become picky analyzers—veritable connoisseurs—of the worship service. Like someone sampling cheeses, we turn up our noses if the flavor isn't just right. We may be real sharp in our spiritual discernment, nailing the problem with the meeting, detailing every flaw in the leadership, and diagnosing the perfect solution. But did we worship? Sometimes we need to intentionally turn off our analyzer and take up our holy calling of ministering to the Lord.

Think about it. What a privilege we have—to minister to God! He owns everything, and all of heaven continually offers Him praise. Is it possible that I could add anything to all that? Amazingly, yes. Scripture reveals that we're able to give something to the One who already has everything. We can bring Him the blessing and praise of an adoring heart. Our affection actually blesses Him! How amazing is that? A creature such as I, ministering to the Lord God Almighty. It's beyond my understanding, but I thrill at the honor. Therefore, I'll take advantage of every opportunity to minister to the Lord of Glory. Let praise arise!

2. To experience God's presence

A second purpose of corporate worship, in this vertical sense, is to encounter God. Said another way, we worship in order *to experience the presence of God*. Let me explain my meaning. The Lord manifests His presence in differing degrees to people. In the most general sense, God is present everywhere and at all times (He is omnipresent). According to Psalm 139:7-10, it's impossible for us to escape His presence. However, even though God is always with us, we don't always sense His presence. Some people go through an entire day without any awareness whatsoever that God is with them. Thus, many people never actually *experience* His presence, even though He's near them.

One way we experience His presence in a more significant

way is by gathering to worship. Jesus said, "For where two or three are gathered together in My name, I am there in the midst of them" (Matt 18:20). He meant that when two or more gather in His name, He manifests His presence among them in a way that is more substantial than His omnipresence. Psalm 22:3 points to this when it says, "But You are holy, enthroned in the praises of Israel." God sets His throne in the midst of His praising people. When we worship together in His name, we can experience more of His grace.

Our hearts long to encounter God. Moses expressed this longing when, on the mountain with God, he begged the Lord, "Please, show me Your glory" (Exod 33:18). The Israelites were about to launch their wilderness trek, and so the Lord promised Moses, "My Presence will go with you, and I will give you rest." Moses responded by saying, "If Your Presence does not go with us, do not bring us up from here. For how then will it be known that Your people and I have found grace in Your sight, except You go with us? So we shall be separate, Your people and I, from all the people who are upon the face of the earth" (Exod 33:14-16).

What distinguished Israel from all the other nations? God's presence. And the very same thing distinguishes the church from the world. *The presence of God is the earmark of the church.* God's presence distinguishes our gatherings from that of a Rotary Club or a community service organization. The folks in those clubs may be happy; they may have fun fellowship and strong relational support; they may enjoy eating and drinking together. But there's one thing they don't have—*the presence of God.* If we don't have God's presence in our services, we may as well shut the whole thing down and throw a picnic instead. We gather in worship because we want God. Lord, we want Your presence to be so strong among us that it's unmistakable even to unbelievers who visit our meetings.

During Jesus' ministry, Luke 5:17 says, "The power of the Lord was present to heal them." In the presence of God the power of God is revealed. As God's presence is realized among worshipers, we can expect to experience His power. Watch for deliverance, cleansing, healing, and baptisms of fire when God is present in power. Where worship is absent, power will also be absent. I once read that when a certain church experienced problems with its electrical system, the following ironic notice appeared in the church bulletin: "Due to the lack of power, there will be no worship service tonight." Maybe the flip of that is equally possible—"Due to the lack of worship, there will be no power in our service tonight." Our hearts long for Jesus to be so present in our worship that His power is released among us.

3. To release spiritual graces

A third reason for congregational worship, in this vertical sense, is *to provide an atmosphere or seedbed for the exercise of the gifts of the Spirit* and various spiritual ministries. I'm not suggesting that our praises convince God to release His gifts in the assembly. But a worship service will provide an atmosphere that is conducive to the release of the gifts of the Spirit (such as those mentioned in 1 Corinthians 12:7-11). We have learned that in an atmosphere of worship, the Holy Spirit seems to move more freely.

For instance, prophecies or spiritual songs rarely come forth at the beginning of worship services. First we worship, then spiritual graces begin to flow. That sequence isn't accidental. It's not as though God has nothing to speak prophetically to His people at the outset of the service; it's just that we're usually not ready yet to receive what He might say. As our spirits become sensitive to the Spirit of God in worship, we become ready to flow in the gifts of the Spirit.

4. To commune with God

Finally, we worship *to open up the channels of communication between us and God.* When we dress nicely for a meeting, our nice attire can mask how distant some of us feel from God. For some, it's been several days since we talked with God. Some may have forgotten to read their Bibles all week.

In their prayerlessness, the enemy may have chewed them up with his accusations. When they come to church, some believers are harassed, disengaged, depressed, or feeling distant from God. The worship service is their opportunity to find new strength in the presence of God. God's house is a house of prayer—a place to connect with God.

When it comes to our daily relationship with Jesus, some of us can be rather incommunicative. But even when the cares of life have choked our spiritual vitality, the Lord still longs for our time and attention. That's why He calls to us, "O my dove, in the clefts of the rock, in the secret places of the cliff, let me see your face, let me hear your voice; for your voice is sweet, and your face is lovely" (Song 2:14). With longing He beckons His dove, His bride. Like a dove, His beloved is sometimes nervous, easily frightened, and hiding in rocky clefts. Even though we've come to the congregation, we still hide our hearts from Him, uncertain of His acceptance. So He pleads with us, "Let Me see your face, let Me hear your voice." Hear Him calling, "Show Me your face!" We hang our heads low in the worship service, burdened with cares and concerns. He wants to lift our heads (Ps 3:3). And He adds, "Let Me hear your voice!" Some are afraid to lift their voice above a whisper, more aware of their insecurities and the eyes of others than the eyes of God. But God delights to hear our voices. He longs for us to lower our guard, lift our face, and give expression to our love in His presence.

We've looked at four things that happen when we connect vertically with Jesus in corporate worship. This is the primary purpose of praise and worship—to connect vertically with the Lord. But it doesn't stop there. Another marvelous purpose of corporate worship involves our horizontal interaction with other worshipers. Let's look at some of those horizontal dynamics.

HORIZONTAL DYNAMICS

I'm a big fan of the secret place and I've written a lot about it. But there's something lacking in the secret place that is fulfilled in the congregation. When we gather to worship, there's a fellowship and camaraderie and synergy that fuels faith and empowers love. It's fantastic to connect vertically with Jesus; but it's also wonderful to connect horizontally with other believers.

I see at least six ways in which worshipers interrelate in the context of congregated praise and worship.

1. To foster unity

First of all, we worship together in order *to enhance unity within the body of Christ*. Unity in the body of Christ is important to the Lord, seen in passages such as Psalm 133 and John 17. Praise and worship are holy catalysts designed by the Lord to strengthen and express our unity.

The unified assembly of saints is a statement in a geographic region and a statement before evil principalities and powers. It's a declaration in the spirit realm that the church of Jesus Christ is alive and well, and the kingdom of God is advancing in our region.

Singing unifies a group in mind, activity, and purpose. When a group sings a song together, they coalesce around a commonly shared message and vision. This explains why singing brings such a valuable contribution to worship. When we sing the same words and share the same passionate focus, our hearts are joined together for the cause of Christ and His kingdom.

This is one reason why believers from different denominations and streams will sometimes gather in an ecumenical convocation to worship together. When we want to gather around the things that unify us, we can't always talk about doctrine because sometimes it's our doctrinal distinctives that distinguish us. But there's one thing we can all agree upon: God is great! We can join together in singing the glorious praises of our Redeemer. The love of Christ is the one thing we all have in common, and we can express our mutual faith in song. When we do, we catch a glimpse of the ultimate song that will rally us around the throne of God.

When you pray and praise with someone, your heart is joined to that person. When we hear someone next to us expressing the depths of their hearts to God in worship and prayer, we discover the rapport we have with them. Our hearts leap within us. *This is my brother! This is my sister! These are worshipers indeed! They're after the same thing I'm after. They long for Jesus like I do.* After a time of worshiping like that, you just want to go around and embrace everyone because you revel in the holy bond that joins your hearts together in Christ.

This is why "praise from the upright is beautiful" (Ps 33:1), because when we lower our guard in the congregation and express ourselves transparently in the presence of others, our hearts are joined to one another. Worship is not open-faced only to God, but also to our brothers and sisters in Christ. There's a level of unity that is found only in being completely open before both God and His people.

2. To minister to one another

A second purpose of corporate worship, in a horizontal sense, is to provide opportunity *to minister to one another.* John seemed to have this in view when he wrote, "And this commandment we have from Him: that he who loves God must love his brother also" (1 John 4:21). When we gather to worship, we go beyond the song, and our hearts begin to reach toward others. We want to pray for someone else, or inquire into their welfare, or share an encouraging word with them. The proof of our love for God finds expression in our care for one another. When the body of Christ is joined together because of what each member supplies, it "causes growth of the body for the edifying of itself in love" (Eph 4:16). Therefore, we come to the worship service not only to receive but also to give to one another.

One way we minister to each other is by inspiring one another to praise. Just as the cherubim of Ezekiel 1:13 have torches of fire passing back and forth between them, believers experience an exchange of fire in worship. We literally ignite one another. When my fire joins with your fire, corporate worship turns into a veritable *bonfire*.

3. To proclaim truth

Third in this horizontal sense, we praise in order *to teach and reinforce spiritual truth*. Paul said that, when we worship, we are, "Speaking to one another in psalms and hymns and spiritual songs, singing and making melody in your heart to the Lord" (Eph 5:19). In another place, Paul said, "Let the word of Christ dwell in you richly in all wisdom, teaching and admonishing one another in psalms and hymns and spiritual songs, singing with grace in your hearts to the Lord" (Col 3:16). Paul made this horizontal function of praise very plain. He said we speak to and teach one another in the songs we sing.

In many of our songs, we address one another. "Sing with me, how great is our God." "Come, now is the time to worship." "Shout to the Lord, all the earth, let us sing." When you analyze the lyrics in our songs, you realize that many of them have us exhorting one another to lift God's praises. And it's absolutely fitting to do so—to spur each other to praise.

Our songs contain troves of biblical truths. As we sing them, our kids gain greater understanding of God and His word. This is especially true when the Scriptures are set to melody. Singing Scripture is an amazingly effective way to help our families memorize and learn the Scriptures. My brother, Sheldon, has said that the songs we sing are in essence teaching our children the practical theology of the church.

4. To confess Christ

A fourth horizontal purpose for praise *provides believers with an opportunity to profess their faith before others*. Congregational praise helps us become more vocal in expressing our faith, because praise is simply a vocal affirmation of our love and faith in Christ. Jesus said that, if we own Him before people, He'll own us before the angels (Luke 12:8). If we lack the courage to confess our solidarity with Christ in the congregation, it's unlikely we'll declare our loyalty before unbelievers. But when we lift our voice before believers, we gain the strength and courage, by His grace, to vocalize our faith before unbelievers.

5. To advertise His fame

The fifth point is related to the fourth, for we praise in the congregation *to declare the glories of God before unbelievers.* When unbelievers visit our worship services, they watch us carefully and listen to every word. We're under scrutiny in our worship services! What impression do sinners get when they listen to our praises and look around the room? Do they look at our faces and think, "I've got enough problems of my own already, without joining up with this morbid bunch"? Or do they witness an authenticity of joy and delight that convinces them our faith is real? May they be struck with the power and grandeur of the God whom we worship!

When unbelievers come to our worship services, we want them to experience the presence and glory of God. Even if they don't understand everything they see and hear, may they realize they're in His presence. It's good to explain to the uninformed why we praise the way we do, to help them with the things they might otherwise misunderstand. But at the end of the day, more importantly than understanding our praises, we want them to experience the reality of the One we praise.

Psalm 108:3 declares, "I will praise You, O Lord, among the peoples, and I will sing praises to You among the nations." God never intended His praises be confined to the ears of believers. Someone might think, "I'm not going to invite my neighbor to our Sunday service because our church really gets energized in worship and I don't want my neighbor to get turned off." Listen folks, we have nothing to be bashful about. I'm suggesting a worship service can be the *best* place to bring an unsaved friend. Why? When God manifests His presence in the midst of His people, unbelievers can be apprehended by the power of the Holy Spirit and drawn to the Lord.

In some churches you wonder if they might be checking ID cards at the door to make sure all who enter are Christians (smile). Then, when all the believers are huddled, the door is locked, the shades pulled down, and the praise service is started. *No!* Throw wide the doors, lift the shades, open the windows, crank the sound, and sing His praise before the whole world!

Praise is evangelistic. It draws people to God. Marketing people know that advertising works. Praise is God's advertising campaign. It's one way we declare our faith before the world. We're telling them of God's goodness, faithfulness, righteousness, mercy, and love. If anybody needs to know about that, it's the uninformed.

6. To prepare for the word

As a final consideration of worship's horizontal dynamics, we find that praise and worship *foster receptivity for the word*. I've asked pastors across the nation, "Do you find it easier to preach after your people have opened in worship?" The answer has invariably been *yes*. People come to the house of God hungry and thirsty. After drinking at the river of God in worship, they're ready to be fed from the word of God. Perhaps we can see this in the words of David, "You visit the earth and water it, You greatly enrich it; the river of God is full of water; You provide their grain, for so You have prepared it. You water its ridges abundantly, You settle its furrows; You make it soft with showers, You bless its growth" (Ps 65:9-10). Just as physical rain enables the earth's crops to grow, the waters of the Spirit soften the human heart and prepare us to receive the implanted word of God. Said another way, worshipers have a voracious appetite for God's word.

Music and worship also fulfill a role in preparing preachers for preaching. The third chapter of 2 Kings tells an interesting story of a harpist being brought to Elisha to calm his troubled emotions. As the harpist played, Elisha's emotions were soothed and he proceeded to prophesy. In a similar way, worship helps preachers and teachers prepare for pulpit ministry. Distractions are quieted and they're able to focus better on the proclamation of the word.

INWARD DYNAMICS

Having looked at the vertical and horizontal purposes of worship, let's now consider what worship accomplishes in us inwardly.

1. Freedom

In worship, we're *liberated on the inside* to give our love to Him with abandon. Worship frees the heart. We find release in the Holy Spirit to offer our affection to Him in a whole-hearted, uninhibited way.

Freedom of heart isn't measured by externals, such as shouting or dancing or clapping. True freedom is a thing of the heart. But when our hearts are free in the Lord's presence, that often translates to freedom of expression on the outside.

The opposite is also sometimes true. When we release our praise externally through such expressions as singing and shouting and clapping, something in the heart can find new freedom at the same time. The heart and body have some kind of interconnectivity.

The worship of heaven will be completely free, uninhibited, and fully engaged from the heart. Since that's where we're going with this thing, why not start now? Let our worship be as pure and transparent as it will be when we're gathered round the throne—on earth as it is in heaven.

2. Articulation

Secondly, corporate worship *gives vocabulary to the feelings of our heart*. All of us have deep feelings for our Savior, but we may struggle at times to find the right words to express those emotions. We get tongue-tied. At such times, corporate worship is really helpful because it empowers us to articulate to the Lord how we're really feeling. Our songs were written by poets and wordsmiths—both ancient and contemporary—who were especially skilled at expressing themselves with lyrics and melody. When we sing their songs, we're empowered to express things to the Lord we've always felt but just didn't know how to say. Thank God for psalmists like King David and Charles Wesley and Chris Tomlin, whose songs have become a tremendous heritage for us. Feelings find vocabulary, words are joined to an enhancing melody, and our hearts soar in praise to God.

3. Faith

Thirdly, *worship increases our faith.* Our songs remind us of the greatness of God's name, works, and power. When the lyrics we're singing declare that nothing is impossible with God, something in our internal chemistry changes and aligns with that truth. Something inside goes, "That's right! Our God can do anything!" As the truths in the songs take root in our hearts, confidence soars.

Paul wrote of this dynamic when he said, "Faith comes by hearing, and hearing by the word of God" (Rom 10:17). When we sing the biblical truths in our songs, our hearts hear those truths in a fresh way and faith naturally begins to rise. The more we sing it, the more faith can abound. The next time you come to a worship service, just watch: Your faith will be strengthened!

4. Holiness

A fourth way that worship affects us on the inside is that *it brings us into holiness.* I think of holiness as the summation of every superlative quality God has in His being. When we can no longer find words to describe His greatness, we're left with just one word: Holy! When we worship Him in the beauty of holiness, His holiness actually rubs off on us. We become holy as we spend time in His presence.

5. Change

Fifth, worship *changes us* into the image of Christ.

Psalm 115 talks about the false gods of the heathen who cannot see or smell or walk or talk. It then adds that "those who make them are like them" (v. 8). Idol worshipers become more like their dead idols. And the same is true of true worshipers. When we worship the living Christ, we come alive and become more like Him. Here's the principle of Psalm 115:8: We become like that which we worship.

It's been said, "You are the company you keep." When we spend intimate time with Him we become like Him. Have you ever seen a couple that was married so long they begin to walk alike, talk alike, and even look alike? I want to hang out with Jesus in loving adoration until I walk like Him and talk like Him.

Paul affirmed that worship transforms us on the inside when he wrote, "But we all, with unveiled face, beholding as in a mirror the glory of the Lord, are being transformed into the same image from glory to glory" (2 Cor 3:18). When we worship, we behold the Lord's glory and are changed, little by little, into His glorious image. True worship actually makes us more like Jesus.

"Well, I don't feel like worship changed me," someone might say. "I left the service the same as when I entered." If worship didn't change you, then ask yourself this question: *Did I unveil my face before God?* If you'll pour your heart out to God with tears of contrition and longing—with an unveiled face—you will most certainly will be changed in His presence.

6. Lifestyle

Sixth in this inward sense, congregational worship *empowers a life of worship*. None of us wants worship to be merely a thirty-minute window we experience on Sunday mornings. Rather, we want worship to be a 24/7 fiery reality in our everyday lives. But sometimes we get weary, distracted, and beaten up in the world. The congregation is a place of healing and renewal. When we leave the service, we're ready to face the storm. Our strength is renewed and our passion for Jesus is revitalized. We're ready again, in the grind of daily life, to make all of life a praise to Jesus.

7. Preparation

Finally, worship *prepares us for new things in God*. God is always doing new things (Isa 43:19), and He wants us to remain fresh and current with what He's doing in the earth. Worship softens our hearts and helps us keep pace with the new things God wants to do.

Praise and worship have preparatory effects. Worship sensitizes our spirits so that when God moves we can recognize it and move with Him. When God does something new, it often comes in an unconventional or unexpected form. If we are not closely attuned to the Holy Spirit, we can easily reject the new thing God wants to do. But if we'll behold Him steadfastly in worship, we'll see when He moves and we'll follow hard after Him.

In this chapter, we've looked at the purpose congregational worship serves in connecting us with God vertically, fulfilling the horizontal functions of worship, and changing our hearts inwardly. These are some of the main reasons we emphasize worship so strongly in our local churches. Worship is powerful! May God's purposes be fulfilled in your church as you worship Him in spirit and in truth.

CHAPTER 7

MOVING PROPHETICALLY IN PRAISE AND WORSHIP

When we worship, the movements of the Holy Spirit among those present increases—within individuals, and throughout the group. As His movements increase, our awareness of His movements also increases. We're aware that the room is catching winds of divine energy. Worshipers are tenderized to hear the whispers of the Spirit and to perceive "what the Spirit says to the churches" (Rev 2:7). When we testify to what the Spirit is saying about Jesus, we're sharing in the "spirit of prophecy" (Rev 19:10). Praises for Jesus become prophetic declarations. The spiritual gifts we've received (1 Cor 12:4-11) are naturally stirred and are more easily expressed. Said another way, when a spirit of worship takes over a room we could also call it a spirit of prophecy.

In this chapter, I'd like to explore some of the ways we move prophetically when we worship. Sometimes prophetic declarations are sung or spoken. Some churches explore the prophetic release of interpretive dance during worship. Many churches flow in spontaneous songs during times of worship. We desire for the Holy Spirit to have the freedom to move among us He desires, with the intended end that we come away from the meeting strengthened in our faith and ignited in greater love for Jesus.

I realize that every local church has its own style, preferences, and protocols. So just apply what is shared in this chapter in any way it strengthens worship in your local church, and just overlook whatever the Spirit tells you to overlook.

What do we mean by our chapter title, *moving prophetically in praise and worship*? Hopefully the following statement can serve as a helpful definition: *To move prophetically in worship is to move with an awareness of the desire and leading of the Holy Spirit, moment by moment, to discern the direction of the Spirit, and to help God's people participate in it.* We long to be led by the Spirit as we worship (Rom 8:14). When I speak of moving prophetically in worship, I am not thinking primarily of someone lifting their voice in the congregation and speaking a prophetic oracle. That kind of expression may be valid in certain contexts, but here we are speaking of our desire to discern the way of the Spirit in the midst of the worship service and then help God's people connect to that.

One way a worship leader can function prophetically, when the saints seem to be disengaged or distant in a particular worship service, is to discern in the Spirit what the problem might be, and then cooperate with the Spirit to surmount every hindrance. In some services, we need a kingdom key from the Lord to unlock what the Spirit wants to do. Worship leaders seek to cultivate a prophetic anointing that enables them to discern the mind of the Spirit and lead a congregation into a dynamic release of encounter with God.

God provides for those involved in music leadership to function under a prophetic anointing. But even more than that, I believe He desires for the entire congregation to participate in prophetic worship. So let's talk about it.

PROPHETIC WORSHIP

What do we mean by *prophetic worship*? Simply put, we mean talking with the Lord. The prototype for prophetic worship is in the book of Genesis, when the Lord God came to the garden of Eden in the cool of the day to commune with Adam and Eve (Gen 3:8-9). They talked *to* Him and also *with* Him. Worship has always been designed by God to be more than a monologue of our telling Him how we feel about Him. He also wants to talk back. He has more on His mind than we do. Worship is an exchange or dialogue—it's two-way communication.

The language of worship is love, and love is an exchange or interchange. This is true in marriage, where love is not a one-sided monologue but an intimate conversation where both spouses express their feelings. This is also true in our relationship with Christ. He loves us first, and then He empowers us to love Him back. In love there is always give and take, talking and listening, expressing and receiving.

The Holy Spirit didn't stop talking once the canon of Scripture was complete. He's still speaking to the church as much as ever—through the word, through the exercise of spiritual gifts (1 Cor 12-14), through inner promptings, and in various other ways. The ministry of music wants to connect with that reality. We want to hear from God.

In some churches, worship is too one-sided. The bride expresses herself to the Lord, but little room is made for the Bridegroom to reciprocate. We want this to change. For worship to be complete, there must be both giving and receiving. Worship's potential is unlocked when we value the relationship between praise (us speaking) and prophecy (God speaking).

I wonder if, from heaven's perspective, some of our worship services look something like this: We sing and shout and praise and clap and worship—and then we suddenly stop and sit down. I almost imagine God waiting with bated breath, hoping for a chance to respond. He also has things to say, but sometimes we don't give Him a chance. Are our service schedules too tight for that sort of thing? And if Sunday morning isn't the right time for that, do we have a time that is?

THE SCRIPTURAL LINK BETWEEN MUSIC AND PROPHECY

There's a symbiotic relationship between music and prophecy, and David explored it intentionally. He and his cabinet appointed musical Levites "who should prophesy with harps, stringed instruments, and cymbals" (1 Chr 25:1). The passage says they were the ones "who prophesied with a harp to give thanks and to praise the LORD" (1 Chr 25:3). Their thanks and praise flowed like inspired oracles. Were they prophesying while musical instruments were being played? Or was the very playing of their instruments an expression of prophecy? I believe the answer is, *both.* They sang prophecies, and they also prophesied upon their instruments.

Musicians can prophesy, therefore, with their voices and also with their instruments. How does prophesying on an instrument work? When musicians are sensitive to the leading of the Holy Spirit, they can play their instrument in a way that opens the hearts of the congregation to more of God.

An anointed musical interlude, played spontaneously in the Spirit at a strategic moment, can sometimes carry more impact than spoken or sung words. I've been in services where a drummer played an unexpected drum solo in such a Spirit-inspired way that it broke the meeting open.

Actually, the link between music and prophecy predated David, seen initially in the time of King Saul. When Samuel anointed Saul to be king over Israel, he told him of several signs that would happen that day to confirm his divine calling as king. Here's how Samuel described one of those signs: "After that you shall come to the hill of God where the Philistine garrison is. And it will happen, when you have come there to the city, that you will meet a group of prophets coming down from the high place with a stringed instrument, a tambourine, a flute, and a harp before them; and they will be prophesying. Then the Spirit of the Lord will come upon you, and you will prophesy with them and be turned into another man" (1 Sam 10:5-6).

That's exactly how it happened. Saul was met by a band of musicians who were coming from a place of worship, and they were playing their instruments as they walked along. The Holy Spirit was resting upon them, and a group of prophets were prophesying as the instruments were being played. The intensity of the Spirit's leading probably ebbed and flowed, perhaps moving from soft to intense and then back to soft. The prophets were probably extolling the Lord in praise, perhaps at times singing known songs and at other times singing spontaneous lines of the moment. When Saul met up with this band of musicians and prophets, the Holy Spirit came upon him and he joined in, prophesying right along with the other prophets. This experience changed him "into another man." What a holy moment!

From there, we can begin to trace the biblical legacy of music and prophecy. It exploded in David's time, and then surfaced again in the ministry of the prophet Elisha. Let me tell the story. In Elisha's day, the kings of Israel and Judah united their armies and went to war. Joram, king of Israel, was ungodly in the eyes of the Lord, and Jehoshaphat, king of Judah, was an upright man. Together, they decided to attack Moab. But before engaging in battle, Jehoshaphat asked if they could consult a prophet of the Lord. One of Joram's servants said that Elisha was nearby, so the two kings went to visit Elisha.

When Elisha saw Joram, the ungodly king of Israel, his soul was disturbed, and he said, "As the Lord of hosts lives, before whom I stand, surely were it not that I regard the presence of Jehoshaphat king of Judah, I would not look at you, nor see you" (2 Kgs 3:14). Elisha was agitated, indignant, and probably even angry. To him, Joram was a scoundrel, and he didn't mind saying so. And now these two kings wanted him to prophesy!

How could he prophesy while so agitated? He needed a way to quiet his spirit. So what did he do? He said, "But now bring me a harpist" (2 Kgs 3:15). Elisha knew that as a gifted musician played the harp, his soul would calm, his heart would become more responsive to the stirrings of the Holy Spirit, and the prophetic gift would flow more easily.

Sure enough. As the harpist played, the hand of the Lord came upon Elisha, and he began to prophesy about the stunning victory God was about to give them over the Moabites. Clearly, the musician used his gift to release Elisha's prophetic anointing. That's why we're saying music and prophecy go together.

Asaph, who was possibly the most senior music minister in David's tabernacle, was called a seer (2 Chr 29:30). Seer was another name for a prophet. As a musician and worship leader, Asaph also functioned as a seer or prophet. He was both musician and prophet. His music ministry functioned under a prophetic anointing. His example demonstrates that today's music ministers can also seek to flow in a prophetic anointing. Excellent musicianship is a marvelous help in a local church, but it's not enough for corporate worship; there must also be an anointing of the Holy Spirit. Today's music ministers must be more than capable musicians; they must also be anointed stewards of the Lord's presence.

Let's go one step further. If God has called someone to a music ministry—such as a singer, worship leader, or musician—let me suggest that God has also called that person to function prophetically. They may not use that language for it, or may not yet be awakened to it, but the calling is there. When God calls someone to the ministry of music, He equips and enables them to perform that ministry.

THE SONG OF THE LORD

We're not the only ones who sing. The Bible tells us that God also sings. Zephaniah 3:17 says He rejoices over us with singing. The Revised Standard Version renders it, "He will exult over you with loud singing as on a day of festival." When we sing to Him, Zephaniah has Him singing back to us. This is the song of the Lord.

Furthermore, when we're gathered to praise God, Jesus joins in. Jesus Himself said so when He said to His Father, "In the midst of the assembly I will sing praise to You" (Heb 2:12). (In that quote, Jesus was speaking prophetically to His

Father through David's pen in Psalm 22:22.) When we gather to worship, Jesus joins in the singing. This also is the song of the Lord.

By the way, did you know Jesus is a Songwriter? Revelation 15:3 says the saints will sing a song co-written by Jesus and Moses. I would love to be in the room when Jesus and Moses sit down together at an instrument and hammer out the tune and lyrics to that song!

So the Father sings (Zeph 3:17), Jesus sings (Heb 2:12), and we sing. One way that prophetic song functions is that someone might begin to sing, in faith, *the song of the Lord* that they believe the Father or Jesus is singing in that moment. As the bride sings her love to Jesus, a prophetic spirit might come upon a singer and they might begin to sing a song as though Jesus Himself were singing back to His bride. Prophets often spoke in the first person, representing the Lord's voice by faith. In a similar way, a prophetic singer might occasionally sing a song in the first person, a song coming from the heart of Jesus to His people.

In whatever manner prophetic song might be expressed, the idea is that we sing to Him, and He sings to us. Prophetic song carries the idea of conversation between the Bridegroom and the bride.

PSALMS, HYMNS, AND SPIRITUAL SONGS

Paul referred twice to *psalms, hymns and spiritual songs* (Eph 5:19; Col 3:16). What did he mean by those designations?

By *psalms*, Paul meant the singing of Scripture. That would especially include singing from the Book of Psalms which was the early church's hymnal. We maintain the same practice today. Many of our songs are Scripture set to contemporary tunes. Every time we sing Scripture, we are fulfilling what Paul intended with his word *psalms*.

What Paul meant by *hymns* is a little awkward to explain because of our modern associations with the word. When we think of hymns today, we think of an old anthem that has three or four verses, followed by a chorus, and is preserved in a hardbound hymnal. Paul had no such idea in his mind, however. Why not? Because anthems didn't exist as an art form until many centuries after Paul.

What exactly did Paul mean, then, by his term *hymns?* He was referring to songs of human composition. When a composer writes a song that is rooted in biblical truth but the lyrics aren't a direct scriptural quote, then we call it a *hymn.* Most songs in church hymnals are *hymns* as Paul meant them, but so are most of our contemporary songs. For example, Chris Tomlin's *How Great Is Our God* is a hymn according to our criteria. Churches that sing the latest worship songs are usually singing hymns.

By *spiritual songs,* Paul was referring to spontaneous songs of the moment that agree with Scripture and are carried along by the Holy Spirit. *Spiritual songs* include what we're calling prophetic songs. But before we talk about spiritual songs, let me say a few more things about hymns.

ABOUT HYMNS

As already stated, in order to fulfill the biblical mandate to sing hymns, all you have to do is sing a sacred song written by a sincere believer, even if the song was written just last night. It doesn't have to be over one hundred years old to be a hymn.

Does this mean we should stop singing the old anthems of the church? No. There are good reasons to keep some of the historic songs of the faith. Let's look at a few.

First, they give us a valuable link to our rich Christian heritage. We have much to gain from those who have gone before us. Only arrogant ignorance would cast a belittling eye toward the songs that have carried believers in generations past. Their songs mined the depths of authentic spirituality, and contribute something we need in our diet. Many hymn writers of previous centuries were, like today's songwriters, skillful in equipping believers with fitting language for worship.

Second, hymns that have survived the centuries tend to

be exceptionally rich in content. They provide a depth of expression that enriches worship by engaging the mind and heart. For example, when a song like Martin Luther's *A Mighty Fortress Is Our God* serves the church for five hundred years, you realize it has an enduring message. Any song that's still widely sung hundreds of years later is likely to strengthen and enrich the vocabulary of your church's worship. Sometimes there's a connection between the strength of a song and its permanence.

Third, some ancient anthems are magnificent carriers of theology. When our children sing them, they learn important things about God and His word.

Fourth, yesterday's hymns can broaden the themes of today's worship services. With some searching, a hymn can be found to support almost any Christian theme imaginable. For example, when a worship leader is searching for a song to support a specific sermon theme, a great place to look is among one's collection of old hymnals.

It's not that unusual for some who love the old anthems of the church to be critical of today's contemporary hymns. This reminds me of the prominent American clergyman who compiled the following ten reasons for opposing the new music trend of his day:

1. It's too new, like an unknown language.

2. It's not so melodious as the more established style.

3. There are so many new songs that it is impossible to learn them all.

4. This new music creates disturbances and causes people to act in an indecent and disorderly manner.

5. It places too much emphasis on instrumental music rather than on godly lyrics.

6. The lyrics are often worldly, even blasphemous.

7. It is not needed, since preceding generations have gone to heaven without it.

8. It is a contrivance to get money.

9. It monopolizes the Christians' time and encourages them to stay out late.

10. These new musicians are young upstarts, and some of them are lewd and loose persons.

These ten reasons are adapted from a 1723 statement directed against the use of—hymns! What we view as the proven anthems of the church were sometimes criticized in their day. Those who are critical of today's hymns inherit their discontent from a long line of predecessors. The controversy has been with us for centuries. For example, in 1984 when *choruses* were popular in worship, a class of Bible college students supplied me with ten reasons why they didn't support the use of old hymns:

1. Many hymns are doctrinal and instructional in nature, rather than contributing to praise and worship.

2. The music is formal, structured, and outdated, as opposed to being youthful and contemporary.

3. Many of the words are archaic.

4. Some have forsaken hymns as a part of their break with the dry deadness of their traditional background.

5. Many hymns *are* dead.

6. Many churches cannot afford hymnals.

7. Hymns represented the new move of God in their day, and choruses represent the new move of God in our day.

8. Choruses are simple and easy to concentrate on.

9. Having to hold a hymnal is a negative factor.

10. Choruses lend themselves more easily to flowing in the Spirit.

Perhaps you can tell from those ten reasons that each generation tends to have its own particular lens for viewing its spiritual heritage. Sometimes the lens is a bit tainted. Is ours?

When commending the *Methodist Hymnal of 1780* to his constituency, John Wesley endorsed it by saying, "Large enough to contain all the important truths of our most holy Religion...In what other publication of this time have you so full and distinct an account of scriptural Christianity? Such a declaration of the heights and depths of religion, speculative and practical? So strong cautions against the most plausible errors? And so clear directions for making our calling and election sure: for perfecting holiness in the fear of God?" Hopefully we can still say the same thing about today's hymns.

There are ways to make yesterday's songs compatible with today's musical styles. For example, some songwriters are picking up old hymns and preserving the lyrics, but giving the music and melody a contemporary feel. Creative rhythms are added, while the melody might be altered slightly or entirely. Resurrecting old songs by giving them a musical facelift helps to keep us connected to our heritage of faith and infuses our worship with vitality and depth. It's a win-win.

Enough about hymns. Now let's look at Paul's third song category—*spiritual songs* (Eph 5:19; Col 3:16).

ABOUT SPIRITUAL SONGS

Spiritual songs are simply "songs of the spirit"—spontaneous heart songs of the moment. While they can be sung in an unknown tongue (1 Cor 14:15), our focus here is on those sung in our native tongue. They're unpremeditated, extemporaneous, unpolished, and thus sometimes a bit faltering, unrefined, or raw. But at the same time, they can be uniquely passionate and infused with Holy Spirit energy.

Usually spiritual songs are sung by individuals. However, when someone sings a spiritual song on a microphone, sometimes a congregation will catch the line that's being repeated and start to sing along. When a group latches onto a spiritual song in this manner, it can fuel the passion of the moment. At times I've heard this kind of collective spiritual singing produce an effect that reminds me of how John described heaven's worship. In Revelation 14:2, John said he heard a sound "like the voice of many waters."

For years, spiritual songs seemed to be practiced by only a few groups in the body of Christ. But in recent years, spiritual songs have been taking the entire body of Christ by storm. Worshipers are learning to release their own individual, genuine expressions of love to the Lord in the congregation. As we become more fluid and fluent in expressing *spiritual song*, it becomes easy and natural to step over into *prophetic song*.

The charismatic renewal of the 1960s and 1970s saw a resurgence of spiritual songs. Entire congregations often sang spontaneously to one sustained chord. In the 1980s, rhythmic patterns and movements within chords began to be added. In the 1990s, this practice began to spill over from charismatic circles and began to ignite many denominations within evangelical and historic circles. The explosion of spiritual songs in recent decades is truly epochal and glorious. It's a recovery of Davidic worship.

To give you a feel for the 1980s, I'll tell a personal story. One evening I went to a home prayer meeting where it was my responsibility to lead worship. In preparing for the worship time, I could not think of any songs I wanted to sing. I went through my entire list, but not one song grabbed my interest as being the song to start with. So I decided we wouldn't start with a known song. Instead, using the melody of the simple chorus *Alleluia*, we sang our own verses unto the Lord. Since we all knew the tune well, everyone was able to lift their voices in an expression of worship that was unplanned and free. As it turned out, we didn't sing a single psalm or hymn that evening, but only spiritual songs. Our spiritual songs produced a beautiful release of worship in the group, and I learned a valuable lesson: We don't always have to sing *known* songs in order to experience authentic worship. We can sing *spiritual songs*, too.

Today, many worship ministries facilitate the singing of spiritual songs through the use of repeated chord progressions. For example, a simple chord progression might run the length of 16 beats or four measures, and then it's played over and over. A variety of melodies can be sung to that chord progression, and sometimes unique melodies are sung simultaneously by everyone gathered. Learning to use chord progressions in spontaneous worship is not really all that difficult to master. The right youtube or internet search will likely help you see various ways this can work.

Generally, there are two levels of spiritual songs. On the first level, we can sing a spontaneous song of praise to the Lord that is meant for His exclusive enjoyment. On the second level, it's possible for an individual to sing a spiritual song that benefits and edifies the entire congregation.

Let's look more closely at this second level—spiritual songs as sung by an individual for the edification of the congregation. I see at least four ways such songs can be expressed.

In the first and most general sense, a spiritual song can be a song of praise directed to the Lord that is expressed in the hearing of the congregation. The singer may simply be overflowing with thankfulness to the Lord for His goodness and may sense that a song of thanks would be a blessing and inspiration to the entire body. As the Lord's praise is lifted, the congregation is blessed by overhearing the song and adding their amen. Room dynamics might require that it be sung on a microphone (in submission to the policies of the church leadership).

When judging whether such expressions are orderly (appropriate), the general litmus test of Scripture is that it must edify the entire congregation (1 Cor 14:5). If a public expression of praise produces a stronger level of praise in the entire congregation, then we consider it profitable. If, however, the service deflates because of someone's song, then we want to learn from our mistakes.

Secondly, a spiritual song can be a song that's sung from the Lord to His people. Some have called this *the song of the Lord*—a term which we discussed earlier in this chapter. When the Lord is singing over His people, someone with spiritual discernment might sense the Lord's song, and by faith sing it to the congregation. We could call this a prophetic song in the sense that the singer prophetically discerns the song of Jesus in the moment. Sometimes such songs are sung in the first person—for example, "My people, I glory in your praises." In this manner, the Lord is able to sing to His church through a human vessel who carries a prophetic sensitivity.

A third type of spiritual song could be an exhortation from the Holy Spirit that is sung to God's people. According to 1 Corinthians 14:3, prophecies should either edify, exhort, or comfort God's people. They can be spoken, but occasionally they can also be sung. Spiritual songs sung in this manner are a biblical way of moving prophetically in worship.

Fourthly, a spiritual song could conceivably be a reflection of the heavenly song. While being stirred by the Holy Spirit, someone might discern the song that is being sung around the throne of God and reflect that song to the congregation. We want God's will to be done on earth as it is in heaven (Matt 6:10), so we want God's song to be sung on earth as it is in heaven. When heaven and earth join together in the same praise, it's a foretaste of what Paul described in Ephesians 1:10, "that in the dispensation of the fullness of the times He might gather together in one all things in Christ, both which are in heaven and which are on earth—in Him."

I encourage churches to exercise all three kinds of songs that Paul mentions—psalms, hymns, and spiritual songs. And we want to find a healthy balance between all three. I'm persuaded our worship will find its greatest depth when all three—psalms, hymns, and spiritual songs—are intentionally exercised in the local church.

THIS IS FOR EVERYONE!

As we read about singing spiritual songs under Holy

Spirit inspiration, some of us might be tempted to think, "Why, I could never do that! I don't have that kind of prophetic anointing on my life." But you don't have to be a prophet to sing prophetically. A *spirit of prophecy* can come upon you and inspire your singing, if you're willing to recognize it and respond by faith. Revelation 19:10 says, "The testimony of Jesus is the spirit of prophecy." Anyone who testifies of Jesus has that spirit of prophecy resting upon them to some degree. When we testify about Jesus in song, our singing is probably under a spirit of prophecy.

Do all prophesy? 1 Corinthians 12:30 seems to infer *no*. Should all desire to prophecy? Yes, 1 Corinthians 12:31 says we should "earnestly desire the best gifts." So if you've never sung a spiritual song, desire it. Lean into it. Practice it.

After all, it seems this desire is in God's heart for us. I have Numbers 11 in view, when the elders of Israel came apart with Moses and Joshua to seek the Lord. As the Spirit of God came upon these seventy elders, they all prophesied. Two elders, however, were not present at the gathering, but the Spirit came on them while they were in the camp, and they too prophesied. Someone ran to report this to Moses, and Joshua spoke up, "'Moses my lord, forbid them!'" Notice Moses' response: "Are you zealous for my sake? Oh, that all the Lord's people were prophets and that the Lord would put His Spirit upon them!" (Num 11:28-29). Joel may well have had this prayer of Moses in mind when he prophesied the outpouring of the Spirit "on all flesh" (Joel 2:28). Moses' wish has become a New Testament reality because, since the Acts 2 outpouring at Pentecost, God's Spirit has been poured lavishly and indiscriminately upon *all* peoples and nations.

Believe it and receive it! The Spirit of the Lord is upon you!

When I first began to understand the role of prophecy in worship, I wanted Him to use me prophetically but was unsure if He wanted to. So I asked Him, "Do You really want to use me in prophetic song?" I hadn't functioned that way previously, nor had anyone laid hands on me and imparted to me the gift of prophecy. I had never heard a voice from heaven, nor did I feel moved upon by the Spirit in a unique way. So how could I know? Then the Lord directed my attention to the verses that we considered earlier (1 Chron 25:1, 3; 1 Sam 10:5-6; 2 Kgs 3:15-16; 2 Chron 29:30), and I came to realize that since He had called me to a music ministry and had anointed me to lead worship, He also desired for me to sing spiritual songs and have liberty in singing prophetic songs. As my understanding grew, I realized He had *already* given me a prophetic anointing. I simply needed to accept that and begin to exercise it by faith. So I did. I began to function in prophetic song (spiritual songs), and it was confirmed as Spirit-led because of the way it edified the congregation.

TAKE A STEP OF FAITH

I found the principle of Romans 12:6 to be really helpful in releasing prophetic song in my life. In that verse, Paul said that if we've been given the gift of prophecy by grace, we should "prophesy in proportion to our faith." Faith is key. Prophetic utterances are unlocked by faith. The first time you step out to sing prophetically will likely require a huge step of faith on your part. If you have faith for it, then sing! Those who are afraid to exercise that kind of faith may never feel moved upon to sing prophetic songs. God doesn't override our faith and make us prophesy with a thunderbolt. Rather, He gently encourages us to exercise our faith and follow the Holy Spirit's lead. Ultimately, if we are to sing prophetic song, there comes a moment when we take a step of faith.

When we go for it, though, we should be prepared to face the consequences. When we're inexperienced and learning, we shouldn't be surprised or offended if a leader gives us a correction or admonishment. On the other hand, if we wait until we're mature enough to exercise the gift perfectly, we'll never do anything. Growth requires boldness to make mistakes and learn. Chances are, however, that instead of a rebuke we'll receive confirmation and encouragement—if the congregation is edified.

If you take a step of faith and attempt to prophesy in

song, what's the worst thing that could happen? Being rebuked publicly from the pulpit? Once you identify the worst thing that could happen, you might realize the risk of faith is worth it. Personally, I would rather take a chance on what might happen if I am used by God than never take a chance and not be used by God.

No matter how mature you become in your gifting and calling, every time you exercise that calling requires an exertion of faith. We never outgrow faith.

Amos said, "Surely the Lord God does nothing, unless He reveals His secret to His servants the prophets" (Amos 3:7). God's thoughts are beyond number—He has *so* much to say to His people. If you have a lot to say to God, think how much more He has to say to you. Let's give Him opportunity in our services to speak. Worship services should be times of interactive dialogue between the Bridegroom and the bride. That's what prophetic song is all about—giving Jesus opportunity to sing over His people.

SOME GUIDANCE

Let me suggest some practical guidelines for growing in the release of spiritual and prophetic songs.

1. Cultivate intimacy with Jesus

To strengthen your flow of spiritual songs, spend much time with Jesus in the secret place. As we meditate in the word and pray in the Spirit, we refresh and enlarge the well from which we draw. Spiritual songs spring from the reality of a fiery friendship with Jesus. Prayer and prophesying go together. For example, as the elders in Antioch gathered to fast and pray, the spirit of prophecy fell and Paul was sent to the nations (Acts 13:1-3). Like the prophets Elijah and Jeremiah, be a person of prayer.

2. Pursue purity

In Malachi 3:2, the Lord expressed His deep desire that

His Levites bring to Him an offering in *righteousness*. When the fountain we draw from is characterized by righteousness and purity, the flow of the Lord's word increases. His words are absolutely pure (Ps 12:6) and they come from a fountain that produces pure water (Jas 3:11).

3. Follow good order

Paul wrote, "The spirits of the prophets are subject to the prophets. For God is not the author of confusion but of peace" (1 Cor 14:32-33). I see four principles here related to due order. First, we can stifle the prophetic flow and we can release it. Second, we are capable of waiting for the proper timing. Third, we are in control and thus are accountable for what we declare or sing. Fourth, emotions should be controlled.

4. Watch for a word

As you're worshiping the Lord, pay attention to those times when a certain word rises to the top of your heart. You may feel inclined to sing a spiritual song around that word or phrase.

5. Evaluate the impulse

Is the song in your heart something for just you and Jesus, or is it something that would edify the entire congregation? Is this the right moment to release it?

6. Be confident

When you decide to sing out a spiritual song, be strong and clear. In the congregation, if an utterance is *inaudible* it's *invalid*. A valid utterance edifies the entire congregation, so it must be heard by all. Don't wait to have the entire song before you start. As you launch out, the Lord will help complete the song. Don't let fear rob you and the church. Faith is willing to take risks so step forward, learn from your mistakes, and grow.

7. Practice

Yes, you can actually practice spiritual songs. Sing them in your secret place. Cultivate and develop your skill in private. Worship teams can also practice spiritual songs during group rehearsals.

We're admonished, "Do not despise prophecies" (1 Thess 5:20). Honor the role of spiritual songs in the congregation. Don't despise the person for being immature or not doing it perfectly. Every prophetic utterance has weak elements to it (1 Cor 13:9). Rather than despising that which is weak, let's receive what the Holy Spirit is releasing through a willing servant.

Prophetic song releases powerful things in the midst of corporate worship. I talk more about that in my book, *FOLLOWING THE RIVER*. May the song of the Lord flow freely in the church, may the name of Jesus be lifted high, and may the Father be glorified!

Part Two
Leading Praise and Worship

CHAPTER 8

THE ART
OF LEADING WORSHIP

Leading worship is an *art* because it's a learned craft. Worship leaders don't become effective overnight. Just as a preacher improves in communication skills and a teacher becomes effective with experience, a worship leader also improves with time and practice. We're going to look now at some of the dynamics of leading worship and consider ways to increase our effectiveness in ministry.

THE NEED FOR A WORSHIP LEADER

A small group meeting in a home may not necessarily need a worship leader, but for worship to be effective in a group of more than a dozen or so, a leader becomes necessary. The larger the group the more significant the leader's role. Leaders bring focus, direction, and cohesiveness to corporate worship so that the time of singing is purposeful and goes somewhere.

Congregational singing requires that a worship leader be appointed. Without a shepherd, sheep tend to wander aimlessly. Corporate worship will crescendo in unity and vitality only under careful leadership. Leaders plan the sequence of songs so there's flow and progression in worship. It's the worship leader's duty to prayerfully prepare the set list.

Furthermore, a worship leader joins the musicians and congregation into a melodic and rhythmic unit. Rhythmic consistency is essential for a smooth flow in worship, so someone needs to be appointed to set the beginning tempo of each song—whether that person is the worship leader or a musician. The need for tempo leadership in corporate worship is actually quite strong.

QUALIFICATIONS OF A WORSHIP LEADER

Each church should establish for itself the expectations placed upon their worship leaders. Let me list here nine qualifications that I would expect most churches to consider essential in a worship leader.

1. A worshiper

First, the leader must be a worshiper. Having musical skills isn't enough. A leader must demonstrate their own personal and passionate commitment to the praises of Jesus Christ. True worshipers worship whether they're leading or not. A true worship leader worships no matter where they are— whether on the platform, in the balcony, or in the middle of the congregation. Worship leaders must first be worshipers because they can only lead people to places they themselves have gone first. Some folks are appointed worship leaders because they have a nice voice or a good ear for music, or because they like to sing or even to worship. But there's a difference between liking worship and being a worshiper. A worshiper is someone who has learned the daily discipline of submitting to the total Lordship of Christ through all of life's changing emotions and circumstances—a quality that's essential for a worship leader.

2. Maturity

A second requirement is a grounded, proven spiritual

walk. Deacons are to be tested before they serve (1 Tim 3:10). We don't want a spiritual novice leading our worship services.

3. Relationship

Third, a leader should be familiar with the styles and customs of their particular church. Leaders need to understand a church's culture so they can engage the congregation in ways that promote a vibrant engagement in worship.

4. Musicianship

Next, the leader must be musically inclined to a level that is acceptable for that specific church. Generally, the larger the church, the higher the level of musicianship that's needed.

5. Blamelessness

A leader must have a good reputation in the fellowship. If someone is not respected for their daily walk with God and their family life, they will not instantly gain the respect of the people simply by stepping onto the platform.

6. Team player

The leader must be a team player, both with the worship team and the pastoral staff. In most churches, the worship leader is also the worship team leader, and we need someone leading the team who is winsome and gathers followers because of the grace they carry.

7. DNA fit

A leader should feel compatible with the church's theology, doctrine, and government. Further, there must be strong bonds of affection with the pastor and pastoral team. We don't need a situation in which the worship leader doesn't like how the church is being run and rips a hole in the church by leaving in an unsavory way.

8. Commitment

The leader should be firmly committed to this church as their home church. This will mean attending meetings at the church even when special events might be held in another church in the region. Like the pastor, the first commitment is to the home church.

9. Inspiring role model

Finally, we want a worship leader with an enthusiastic, friendly, engaging personality. Leaders need to demonstrate the ability to lead people both on and off the platform. Enthusiasm and zeal for Jesus is contagious. If the leader is socially challenged when mixing with people, the people will struggle to receive their platform leadership.

Qualifications such as these nine are not intended to discourage candidates from becoming worship leaders, but to inspire them to rise to the upward call of Christ. Serving as worship leader is one of the most visible capacities of servanthood in the entire local church. It's fitting, therefore, for the qualifications to be proportionately sober.

Do you desire to lead worship? You desire a noble task, so let your heart rise to the challenge. Let the greatness of the calling motivate you to walk more closely with God.

After meeting these qualifications, a leader will want to continue to grow in every way—in musical skill, in leadership abilities, in spiritual sensitivity, and in the knowledge of Christ. Experience can grow a strong leader into an exceptional leader.

Worship leading is not as much about *doing* as it is about *being*. It's a great compliment when people say, "You're the same on the platform as you are at home." People are not endeared to a leader who assumes a platform personality— that is, an artificial persona—when in front of a crowd. When on a microphone, we don't try to impress people with our stage presence and flowery style. Rather, we display authenticity and sincerity. People want to follow the real you.

While the heart of the worship leader is the most important

factor, certain outward elements must also be considered. God looks on the heart, but people see externals, so dress is a factor. A church's platform dress code should be honored. Worship leaders try to dress in a way that makes them invisible. We can distract people when our attire is overly casual or overly formal. Above all, we should dress modestly.

THE LEADER'S MUSICAL EXPERTISE

While there may be exceptions, usually the Lord calls worship leaders who have a musical ear and an ability to understand fundamentals of music. Musical knowledge will only increase a leader's effectiveness. We want a leader that the musicians on the team enjoy working with.

How can a worship leader keep growing musically? First, develop your singing ability. Take some voice lessons. Learn to increase your vocal projection and control. Try to develop the attractiveness of your singing voice (yes, it can be developed). Work on a pleasant vibrato. Sight-reading melody lines is another valuable and learnable skill.

Sometimes a song can get started in a wrong key by mistake, and people are either singing way too high or way too low in their vocal range. When that happens, no need to sing all the way through the song in the bad key. Stop the song and say something like, "We're in the wrong key. Let's get it right." The musicians will change the key, and away we go.

Rhythmic stability is helpful in worship, which is why click tracks are helping so many worship teams. It's amazing how quickly a wrong rhythm can undermine the effectiveness of a great song. If the song is too slow, people will feel a heaviness on the song. The problem probably isn't a spirit of oppression on the meeting; it's just that the song is too slow. Or if a song is too fast, the people aren't able to absorb the meaning of the song and may even struggle to spit the syllables out fast enough. Wise leaders labor to find the right tempo for every song.

Click tracks will enable you to start a song at its optimum tempo with the very first beat. If you don't have the option of click tracks, develop the skill of starting a song off at the right tempo. Drummers should especially hone this skill.

Drummers should also develop the skill of changing the tempo of a song mid-song. If a song is being sung too slowly, learn how to speed up the tempo. This is harder than it sounds. I had a drummer on my worship team once who, whenever I signaled to him to accelerate the tempo a little bit, just started hitting the drums harder. It was outside his skill set at the time to lead the team into a faster tempo. My point is, it's not easy to do and requires practice. If your drummer doesn't know how to change the tempo in the middle of the song, there's nothing wrong with stopping the song and starting over again. All this can be done graciously without insulting any of the musicians by saying something like, "This sounds like a funeral dirge." We're not placing blame on anyone for the wrong tempo, we're simply giving it another attempt.

A COMMITMENT TO GROW

Worship ministries are always striving to increase in excellence. Why? Because when we're growing in mastery over our instruments, or adding new sounds to the team, or improving our vocal expertise, we're strengthening our ability to lead in a broader range of worshipful expressions. The more diversified a worship ministry is, the better equipped they are to follow the creative movements of the Holy Spirit and serve the diverse needs of the congregation.

Let me illustrate with the example of a car mechanic. Suppose you took your car to a mechanic who owned only a pair of pliers, a hammer, and a screwdriver. He would be rather limited in the kinds of repairs and services he could perform on your car. The more tools at his disposal, the wider the range of repairs he can service. The same principle holds true for a worship ministry. Worship teams are always trying to strengthen their toolkit so they can serve the congregation more effectively.

This is one reason worship teams prepare for worship by constantly learning new songs. Every song a worship team masters becomes another tool at their disposal to make the Lord's praise glorious and to provide believers with language to unlock the heart.

A church's worship ministry is one of the most visible ministries of a local church, and excellence in music is a statement to guests who visit the church. It tells seekers and inquirers that we are committed as a church to excellence in every sphere of our ministry—a quality that is attractive to anyone checking out a church.

Encourage your musicians to take more music lessons. Bring in a vocal coach for your singers. Hold a clinic for songwriters. Train the musicians in music theory and improvisational techniques. Hire a sound consultant. Send helpful Youtube clips to everyone on your team. Read and discuss a good worship book together. Build a mechanism to train young musicians in the church. Let's keep growing!

GENERAL GUIDELINES FOR LEADERS

Be dependable. When you're prepared, prompt, and communicative, you prove yourself a strong asset to the pastor and the leadership team. Be true to your word and cultivate faithfulness. Fulfill your pastor's expectations. Show yourself to be a humble and diligent servant of Christ.

Be natural. Be true to yourself when leading worship. Don't imitate the style of another worship leader. Glean from other worship leaders, but then adapt what you learn to your own personality. People will enjoy following you when they see that you're comfortable in your own skin. The body needs you to be you.

Ride a wave all the way to the shore. By saying that, I'm using surfing language. A surfer will search and wait for a wave to ride. Once they find the right wave and are riding it, they'll stay with that wave for as long as it will carry them. A similar dynamic can happen in a worship service. Sometimes you'll catch a wave of the Spirit and become aware that God is moving in a specific way in the moment. When you sense that special breath of God upon the worship of the moment, be slow to move to the next thing. Take time to enjoy the movements of the Spirit in that place of special intimacy. If you sense the Spirit highlighting a certain theme, such as adoration, repentance, rejoicing, or whatever, be willing to stay there for a few moments. If God is doing a work in hearts, wait for Him to complete that work. What's more important in our service order than meeting with God? He's the reason we've gathered. When He's speaking, let's listen.

On a similar note, don't seat the people in the middle of a groundswell of praise. When there's enthusiastic energy on a song, seating the people is like dumping water on a fire. When you're in high worship, allow the people to stand.

Some services have been occasions for what I once termed *spiritual abortions*: The worship service was called to a halt before God was able to complete what he was trying to birth in the hearts of His people. Look for a confirmation in your heart that the worship service is *finished*.

On the other side of it, avoid *flooding* by singing too many songs or elongating the worship service past its sense of completion. Just as a plant can be harmed by too much water, a worship service can get bogged down by too many songs.

Worship leaders, be ready with a suitable song at all times—"in season and out of season" (2 Ti 4:2). Worship leaders are sometimes called upon to lead a song in the most unexpected moments. So when you're in a meeting, be asking yourself, "If they were to call for an appropriate song right now, which would I choose?" See yourself as always on call. Something pastors love in a worship leader is when they have the ability to pull out a fitting song at a moment's notice.

Be ready to explain. I mean, be prepared to help visitors understand some of the ways we worship. The Holy Spirit may direct you on occasion to give a scriptural explanation for certain expressions of praise and worship. This is not necessary in every meeting, but it can be helpful when done with sensitivity and brevity. You may consider placing a page on the church site that describes your corporate worship services and provides scriptural substantiation for your practices. It can be helpful for people to know what to expect when they visit.

Learn to find the right balance between overly strong and overly weak leadership styles. Soliciting feedback from the leadership team can be helpful here. Be yourself. But if you have a strong personality, exert some restraint in your leadership style. If, on the other hand, your personality is more withdrawn, you may need to exert yourself to provide the strength of leadership a service needs. All of us want to find a leadership style that is clear, inspiring, passionate, and sensitive.

Be passionate in your love for Jesus. People don't follow you because you've arrived; they follow you because you're hungry. They're not inspired by your attainments but by your reach.

Some worship leaders come to services to "do a job"—to get the people to worship. As though it's just another gig. This mentality produces a hireling spirit. Instead of trying to make everyone else worship, why not abandon all that and give yourself to worshiping Jesus in their presence? The sincere will respond to your authenticity and vulnerability. The contagion of your passion for Jesus will ignite a fire in their spirits and inspire them to join your pursuit of Christ.

All worship leaders can do is bring themselves to the meeting. When we lead worship, you get us. No facades—just the real us. Worship leading is *taking your private cry and making it public*. Where are you at, personally, in your walk with God? Bring that to the meeting. Release your cry to God in the presence of the congregation and they'll join you.

THE WORSHIP LEADER/MUSICIAN

I encourage worship leaders to learn to play an instrument, if they're able. This skill is not essential to worship leading, proven by the fact that many effective worship leaders don't play an instrument. But it's helpful. I especially recommend that worship leaders learn to play either the keys or guitar because either instrument is highly conducive to leading worship.

I see at least three benefits to playing guitar or keys while leading worship.

1. Rhythm and tempo

Hand movements on the instrument help to set and maintain the tempo of a song because the movements are both seen and heard. This is easier and more effective in communicating a tempo than choral hand movements or the snapping of a finger. Now the worship leader is in the driver's seat when it comes to setting or changing a tempo.

2. Song transitions

You don't need to signal when the song is over, or announce what the next song will be. Instead, you can just close down the song with your own musical leadership, or you can move seamlessly into the next song without having to announce anything to the congregation or team.

3. Communication

In general, communication is much tighter. For example, if you want to make a musical change, instead of trying to convey verbally to another musician what you're wanting, you can just initiate the change on your own. Instead of saying to a musician, "Give me an A chord," you can supply it yourself.

Sometimes a worship leader wants to communicate something to the musicians but is unable to make eye contact in the moment. In those moments, cues are sometimes delayed or missed. When the worship leader is a musician, many of those cues are communicated fluidly simply by playing on the instrument that which is desired.

Sometimes a worship leader wants a musician to play a

musical interlude, and it can be difficult to convey what is desired. Words can fall short. "Play something intuitive right now." How do you tell a musician what you want? They can't read your mind. But if you can play something yourself, the others can follow.

Playing an instrument while leading worship is challenging. It's a lot to do all at once—sing the melody accurately, stay on pitch, get the lyrics right, play the song in the right key, hit the right chords, set the right tempo, lead the team, read the congregation, discern the Holy Spirit's leading—not everyone is capable of balancing all those things simultaneously. To do so effectively means the worship leader must become so familiar with their instrument that playing it becomes almost second nature to them. But it's amazing what someone can learn to handle with enough practice. Spend as much time as possible singing with your instrument, and you will strengthen your ability to lead from the instrument. The rewards are worth it.

INVISIBLE LEADING

Some congregations have learned to praise in direct proportion to the level of energy exuded by the worship leader. The more the worship leader shouts and dances and exhorts, the more the people respond. But I consider this to be a faulty paradigm. This turns the leader into a herder and the people into performers. Worship is not a response to placate the expectations of the worship leader; it's a response to the gracious movements of the Holy Spirit in the heart. It's a response of love.

Some worship leaders exercise such a visible platform presence that the congregation instinctively keeps their eyes glued to them. Every move is directed from the platform, and the people respond almost automatically. Leaders who maintain this kind of high platform profile can actually distract people from worship. It's hard to see the Lord when the leader is so large.

I'd like to present a paradigm for worship leading in

which the leader provides clear leadership, but also seeks to be as invisible as possible before the congregation. The goal is to get out of the way so the focus of the worshipers moves from the horizontal to the vertical plane.

The entire worship team wants to become invisible, but this goal is not always easy to attain because of the highly visible nature of our ministry. Think about it. The seating is contoured so everyone faces us; we're on a raised platform; there are spotlights on us; they're trying to follow the tune we're singing; the musicians are giving signals to each other; we're giving exhortations and reading Scriptures; everything we're doing is being amplified through powerful audio speakers; we're demonstrating praise and worship by lifting our hands, clapping, dancing, singing, etc. With so much sight and sound coming at them from the platform, how can the people help but be riveted by us?

With such a highly visible position, the onus comes on the entire worship team to strive for the maximum degree of invisibility possible. The service needs direction, so we don't relax our leadership, but we labor to become invisible in the presence of the glory of Christ.

The best way I know for the worship team to become invisible is for each one on the team to set their eyes on the Lord. As we lift our hands and face to the Lord and demonstrate with our body language that we're engaging with Jesus, we cease being something to watch. When the people look at us, their instinctive response is to raise their eyes to the One we're beholding—the Lord Jesus Himself.

Expressive, animated movements can be appropriate for the singers on the platform during energetic praise. But when we progress deeper into worship, we should avoid large movements that draw attention to ourselves.

One way to become less visible is to back away from the microphone a bit when the congregation has their own momentum in the song and doesn't need us to carry every note.

The question has been asked whether worship leaders should keep their eyes open or closed. I think both are permissible, but I personally favor mostly open. I saw a worship leader once who kept his eyes closed during the entire worship service. He may have been connecting with God, but he certainly wasn't connecting with the room. He had no idea where the congregation was at. On the other hand, some worship leaders are continually looking around to see how things are going in every corner of the sanctuary. They're very engaged with the congregation but don't appear to be very connected to the Lord. Worship leaders can fall into the *Martha syndrome* of serving at the expense of worshiping. A leader should look out occasionally to discern the engagement of the congregation but, above all, be looking on the Lord in worship. As a worshiper, therefore, I think it's okay for a worship leader to occasionally close their eyes for a few moments if they want.

THE WORSHIP LEADER'S PRIMARY OBJECTIVE

Worship leaders are pastors of worship. They're shepherds. Worship leaders aren't simply trying to elicit a certain response from worshipers; they're seeking to take the congregation somewhere together. We're on a corporate journey into the heart of God.

In a nutshell, the goal of the worship leader is *to provide the best opportunity possible for the people to worship.* We spread a banquet table, and it's their decision to partake. If they decline to participate, we remain unmoved—we will continue to give them the best opportunity possible. The thinking of worship leaders is something like, "I'm going into the throne room of heaven. You're welcome to join me and the team as we enjoy God's presence. But whether or not you join, we're still going in!" If we're leading a group that is resistant or unresponsive, sometimes we just need to release them to the Lord and go after God for ourselves.

Bottom line, we're not the worship leader. The Holy Spirit is the real Worship Leader. He alone can inspire and move the hearts of people. As a worship leader serving under His administration, we're simply a vessel through whom He operates. If the Holy Spirit is not empowering a certain group to worship, what makes us think we can? When the service we're leading is tough, sometimes we simply relinquish and release the meeting to the sovereign will of the Holy Spirit.

When worship leaders become controlling, it's usually rooted in a noble desire to see the people worshiping freely with an unveiled face (2 Cor 3:18). However, we must continually resist the temptation to implement a God-given vision with natural strength. Sometimes we get impatient with how slowly the people are progressing in their responsiveness to God, and we want to urge them along. But if we try to drive the sheep at a pace faster than the Holy Spirit is setting for them, we can easily begin to strive in the flesh.

Almost every worship leader has to grapple at some point with the propensity to strive in human energy. Technically, we know that it's, "'Not by might, nor by power, but by my Spirit,' says the LORD Almighty'" (Zech 4:6), but still it's so easy to get a step or two ahead of God.

Romans 15:30 speaks of striving in prayer, but worship is different. Worship is a striving-free zone. The priests in Ezekiel's tabernacle wore linen garments in order to minimize sweat (Ezek 44:18). Ministry to the Lord should be *no sweat*. There's a tension here, because some worship leaders will come away from a worship service wet with perspiration. That's because leading worship is sometimes hard work. And yet, there's a repose of spirit the Lord wants leaders to find even in the rigors of worship leading.

Let God give you a grand vision for worship in your local church, but then labor only in the Spirit's power to bring it to pass. Leaders become much more effective when they relax and learn how *easy* Jesus' yoke truly is. Plow in your own strength and you'll exhaust quickly. Learn to flow with the Holy Spirit and He'll do the plowing.

Our goal as worship leaders is not worship. If our goal is worship, we'll focus more on outward manifestations. It's possible to have all the sights and sounds of worship but be empty at the heart level. Our goal isn't worship, therefore, but

God. We have eyes only for Jesus (Heb 2:9; 3:1; 12:2). When He's our goal, we'll worship. Let's be careful lest we *worship worship*—that is, lest our goal becomes physical manifestations of high-energy enthusiasm. We're not pursuing external expressions but a dynamic, spiritual encounter with the living God.

GETTING—AND LOSING—CONTROL

A worship leader doesn't conduct or coerce or cheerlead. Rather, we encourage, prompt, and inspire. When we manipulate or strive to elicit a certain response from the people, we're moving into the forbidden territory of controlling worship. We shouldn't direct the responses of the people, even if the goal is noble. Effective worship leaders learn the art of exhortation, not manipulation. We don't control, we inspire.

If a worship leader isn't a cheerleader, does this mean we shouldn't do anything to awaken the people to praise? Far from it. The leader has a significant role in stirring and stimulating praise. The worship leader's approach can be summarized by this dictum: *get control, then lose control.*

Get control. Exercise your strongest leadership at the launch of the worship service. Step up and take charge. Be strong with your voice and be directive with the songs you're leading. This will help the service get off to a strong start. And this will help the people relax because they will realize the service is in the hands of a leader who will take us somewhere. In other words, don't get up and apologize, "Our regular worship leader wasn't available today, so they called on me. I don't know what I'm doing and, to be honest, I'm scared stiff. If you'll pray for me, I know God will help us get through this." Even if you feel uncertain and incompetent, put your insecurities aside and *lead.* The people will relax and worship if they feel the service has strong, confident leadership.

Call the people to praise. Encourage and provoke with cheerful optimism. Lay hold of the meeting and gather the room. We don't apologize for the fact that God has chosen to use human leadership. God doesn't lead worship services without us; He leads through us. The worship service must be led, and worship leader, that's your role. Lead! If your confidence is lagging, you might even recite Scriptures such as Isaiah 61:1 to yourself, encouraging yourself that the Spirit of the Lord *is* upon you. The people are ready to follow and they're looking for someone to lead.

But then, *lose control*. At some point in the worship service, take your foot off the gas, rescind your ability to manhandle the meeting, and decide in your heart to give room to the Holy Spirit. It's fairly easy to take control of a worship service; it's threatening to our insecurities to surrender that control to the Spirit's lead. Why? Because we don't know what He'll do with it. And yet, this is where worship leading becomes most effective and where running with Jesus becomes most adventurous.

An enthusiastic leader might be able to stimulate an enthusiastic praise service, but no human is capable of empowering people to worship. Only the Holy Spirit can unlock the heart. This is why we lose control to the Holy Spirit. We give Him room to move on hearts in ways we can't accomplish even with our best leadership skills. If we insist upon holding a tight rein on the entire worship service, we can miss the sovereign move of the Spirit.

As long as we maintain control of the worship service, we'll have a man-directed service. When we surrender our control, we open to the possibilities of a Spirit-led worship service. Notice that I didn't say we'll have a *Spirit-controlled* service. Why not? Because the Bible never talks about being Spirit-controlled. It speaks of being self-controlled and Spirit-led. The Holy Spirit will never try to control us but will graciously lead us in worship when we move over and give Him the driver's seat.

The Holy Spirit never controls people, and neither should we. To *get control* means, therefore, that worship leaders don't take control of the *people* but of the *meeting*. And to *lose control* means we give control of the meeting to the Spirit's lead.

What are some ways a worship leader can lose control? The following suggestions might give you a feel.

1. Ask

Stop and talk internally with the Holy Spirit. Ask Him, "What's on Your heart for this moment? Is there anything You want me to do right now?"

2. Withdraw

Back away from the microphone and set your heart upon God. By backing off the microphone and lifting our faces to the Lord, our body language tells the people, "I'm not going to orchestrate what happens next. This service belongs to the Holy Spirit." This will inspire the congregation to give the Lord and His leadership their full attention. When God takes over, all kinds of glorious things can happen. People can be convicted, saved, delivered, healed, and made new in the Lord's presence. Powerful things can be unlocked through a prophecy or spontaneous song or a spirit of prayer resting upon a gathering.

3. Wait

Stall on singing the next song on your set list. Give the Spirit opportunity to do something outside your service preparation. A song might arise from someone on the worship team, or even someone in the congregation. If the Lord triggers something spontaneous like that, you'll be ready to sail with Him in that new direction. You'll be off and running with Him!

4. Bow

Go to your knees. Who says a worship leader can't kneel or fall prostrate during worship? A change of posture like that can produce expectation in the people because they'll realize we're reaching for the Lord.

It's threatening to the ego to lose control because, if the

Holy Spirit doesn't step in and help in a way we can identify, we can appear to be aimless and incompetent in our leadership. Worship leaders are always putting their pride on the altar. We're willing to look bad so the Holy Spirit can have His way.

I would imagine that almost every worship leader has been tempted to control corporate worship. But why should we? Do we think we're the shepherd and know where the sheep need to go? But sometimes we get an end in view and then try to control the congregation until that end is achieved. It's better to admit that we don't know everything God wants to do in worship, and rely upon the Holy Spirit from start to finish to accomplish what He alone can do. The potential of worship is as limitless as God Himself. Only God knows what He can do when we surrender to His leadership. Let's give Him room to work "exceedingly abundantly above all that we ask or think" (Eph 3:20). That awareness may one day lead us to say something like this: "Let's take a little more time to enjoy the Lord's presence as we sing this line again. It's possible that God is doing as many things in this room right now as there are people. Let's take the time to allow Him to complete His work in our hearts." God is always doing more in corporate worship than leaders realize or understand. So get control and then lose control.

THE ART OF EXHORTATION

When a meeting starts, even though we're all gathered in one place there are probably some who aren't ready to worship. They might look ready, but appearances can mislead. Some need help to lower their defenses. Sometimes the sheep arrive to the meeting weary, discouraged, distracted, battling accusatory thoughts, or feeling distant from God. It can take time for them to open to the Lord, and that slow start can test the patience of the worship leader. In that moment, don't whip the people. After all, they've been beat up all week just by living in this world; they don't need another beating. Rather, through gentle wisdom and loving discernment, let's lead them to a place of tender surrender to the Lord.

When leading a congregation forward in worship, one of the tools at a worship leader's disposal is the *art of exhortation*. This tool can be especially helpful when the people are struggling to engage with Jesus. Exhortation is an art to be perfected, just like preaching or teaching. It's a learned ability. If you feel that exhorting is inconsistent with your personality, I won't pressure you. But since God has called you to lead the people in worship, could it be that He wants you to learn all the tools that can help you provide effective worship leadership? A one-sentence exhortation at the right moment can make a difference in a meeting.

Some churches don't permit their worship leader to exhort the congregation during worship, and that's fine. But for those churches that do, let me try to add some helpful perspective.

Exhortation is not coercion nor manipulation, but persuasion. It follows Paul's heart when he wrote, "We persuade men" (2 Cor 5:11). He also urged Timothy, "Teach and exhort these things" (1 Tim 6:2).

Deliver an exhortation with conviction and confidence, just as Peter wrote, "If anyone speaks, let him speak as the oracles of God" (1 Pet 4:11). Be audible to all and enunciate your words clearly so everyone understands you.

Virtually every worship leader has their turn at being frustrated or impatient with the people, usually over their lack of response in worship. Exhortation is not a biblically endorsed way for worship leaders to vent their exasperation. If you're frustrated with the people, don't show it. Rather, bear with them in love. Let every exhortation be an expression of tender care. Hearts will soften in the presence of genuine warmth but harden in resistance if you're impatient or upbraiding.

There may be the rare exception, but generally speaking, don't rebuke or chide the people. Here's why. You have the four seasons in every service. What I mean is, in every service there are people in every season of life. Chances are that some of the worshipers are in the dead of winter spiritually. They've been pruned vigorously by God, and now they stand quivering in the freezing conditions of a hard spiritual winter. It may have taken all their courage just to make it to the meeting. In that moment, they don't need someone to slap their face and tell them to wake up. They need a gracious leader who provides room to breathe and weep and mourn. With every exhortation, be sensitive to those in a difficult season of life.

Sometimes an entire church will go through a winter season together. God orchestrates winter seasons in order to work deeply in a congregation. Even in winter, a tree's roots continue to grow. The foliage in the next summer season will give witness to that inner growth. Don't despise worship winters because they'll be followed, in due time, by new heights of joy.

Save your exhortation for the right moment. Some services take off right from the start, and in such cases, there's no need for an exhortation. But other services struggle to gain momentum, and those are the times when you want to be able to offer an inspiring exhortation.

There are a few ways to exhort. One way is to read or quote a Scripture. Some churches will use a Scripture reading as their call to worship—it's an excellent way to exhort. A worship leader may want to have several Scriptures written down, and then they can pull out any of them whenever the moment seems right. Yes, I'm suggesting a worship leader can plan an exhortation during service preparation. If the Spirit can direct your heart to select some great songs to sing, can He not also direct your heart toward a Scripture to read, or an exhortation to give? If you're like me, you can probably craft a more positive exhortation in your prayer time during the week than trying to create one suddenly in the middle of a service.

Another way to exhort is to lead in a corporate prayer. Just by expressing your heart to the Lord in prayer, a congregation can be moved to join their hearts to yours.

Another way to exhort is to use a prophetic parable or picture from nature. Something you saw in a nature video might inspire worship in the congregation.

Exhortation should function under a Holy Spirit anointing. What I mean is, you should feel a witness in your heart from the Holy Spirit that these are the right words for this moment. When spoken tenderly under the Holy Spirit's guidance, an exhortation can fuel the momentum of a worship service. If you attempt an exhortation that actually deflates the worship service, debrief about it afterwards with your pastor and learn.

Be brief. I've seen some worship leaders, under the banner of exhortation, deliver a sermonette. Wrong. Just lead worship, and let the preacher do the preaching. If you do exhort, say it as succinctly as you can.

If your church is in a season where more services than usual have been tough slogging, then ask this question: Is it time for our pastor to teach the congregation again about praise and worship? Sometimes small exhortations aren't enough; sometimes a congregation needs biblical preaching on this important topic. Corporate teachings on worship are likely to produce good fruit in the collective life of a congregation.

DEALING WITH DIFFICULT TIMES IN WORSHIP

A worship team loves it when the Holy Spirit is "oiling" a service and helping it move forward freely and effortlessly. But sometimes God intentionally takes us through dry times in our worship services. Just as the rigors of exercise make us stronger in our bodies, the rigors of resistance in worship can make us stronger spiritually. God uses tough times to take us deeper in Him.

Sometimes He'll deliberately engineer a *horrible* worship service. Why? Perhaps to keep us dependent upon Him. We can become confident in our preparation, expertise, and team strength, and sometimes we need a reminder that our best is simply not enough. We desperately need the Holy Spirit to move sovereignly in our corporate gatherings.

Understanding that we're dependent on the Holy Spirit to help us through tough services, is there anything we leaders can do to help the service get off the ground? We've already talked about the art of exhortation; what else can we do?

Here's one idea: Pull out a song that takes us to the cross. Why? Because the cross is the genesis and fountainhead of all worship. That's where the passions of worship are excavated. When our hearts place their focus on the cross, worship and thanksgiving are our most natural response.

Here's another idea. Put a pause on the songs, and invite everyone to greet a few neighbors and get their name if they don't know them. Why? Because people tend to be reserved when standing next to someone they've never met. Sometimes a few moments of greeting can help a congregation gain a better sense of connection to one another. When we connect with our unity, we gain a corporate identity and confidence in worship.

Sometimes a worship leader can be fully prepared, both musically and spiritually, and yet find themselves in a worship service that is hard, and they have no idea what to do next. I've noticed two general ways that worship leaders tend to respond to uninspired worship services. Some worship leaders will hunker down and just plow forward. Other worship leaders will pause and go into a seeking and waiting mode, seeking the Lord for direction. There's a time and place for both approaches. I've watched God honor both.

I've been in services where the Lord gave a key that opened wide the worship service; and I've been in services where nothing seemed to help—as though the service was doomed to stay on the ground from the start. In such cases, sometimes you just close down the singing time and move to the next thing on the program. Perhaps the Spirit's release will come through the sermon this week instead of the worship.

Some services start to ebb because the leader has dragged the service out with too many songs. The best answer in such cases is to move on to the next portion of the service.

When you scan the congregation and it appears the people aren't participating, don't trust your eyes. The look on the faces of the people doesn't always accurately reflect what's happening in their hearts. You can look at them and think they're "out of it" when in fact their hearts are very much engaged with the Lord. You can't always tell by the expressions on people's faces whether they're connecting with God because they don't always inform their faces. For example, I remember being part of a worship team in one service in which a certain gentleman scowled at us for the duration of the service. I was convinced he had barely tolerated the entire thing. Afterward, however, he expressed his appreciation more warmly than anyone else. That taught me the important lesson that we cannot always "read" someone's receptivity by the expression on their countenance. Some people can thoroughly enjoy a worship service but look miserable throughout. If the expression on the people's faces discourages you, stop looking at them! Release them to the Lord and set your gaze on Him.

When you find yourself leading a tough worship set and have no idea what to do next, check with the Holy Spirit. He's been given to you as your Helper. Ask for help. "Holy Spirit, is there anything You would have me do right now to lead this worship service forward into Your heart?" You may be surprised at how eager the Holy Spirit is to lead those who call on Him for help. Ask Him to show you what's holding the people back; then ask Him to show you what is needed to help them respond more freely to the Lord. Worship leaders should come to a service with a spirit of prayer already abiding on them so they can discern the Spirit's guidance during the meeting. Above all, worship leaders long to be led by the Holy Spirit (Rom 8:14).

Sometimes the worship service is tough because you personally are in a tough season. What should worship leaders do when we're so troubled that we don't even want to be in the meeting? Be real with the worship team. Tell them where you're at, and ask for their prayers before the service starts.

Then go out and be real in the presence of God. Pursue God in the presence of the congregation. Release your cry to God.

Have you ever seen an eagle or hawk spread its wings and ascend without even flapping? That's because it has found a *thermal*—an updraft of warm, rising air that enables it to soar. Worship services can also catch a thermal—a spiritual updraft in which a service ascends in the Spirit almost effortlessly. Let's labor to find the heart of the Holy Spirit in each service and partner with Him. What a delight when we connect with His movements and rise on eagles' wings!

STANDING IN WORSHIP

In Chapter One, we said it's biblical to stand in worship. He sits, we stand. However, a congregation represents a spectrum of strength and comfort levels. The young ones can stand and jump for an hour straight, while for others it's painful to stand at all. People may want to stand, but after a while they may grow weary. The question is, for how long should a worship leader expect the people to stand during worship?

Some churches have responded by limiting their worship services to a briefer limit of time. But what about churches that want to spend longer periods of time in worship?

One solution is to seat the people strategically during specific segments of the worship service. These times could be planned in advance.

Another solution is to tell the people that they are free to stand or be seated of their own volition. When people are not instructed to rise or be seated, it becomes evident rather quickly, even to guests, that everyone is free to sit or stand at their own pleasure. In my opinion, I think it's good to teach them the biblical value of standing in worship and then leave it to their discretion to sit when they need a break.

Generally, I prefer a church culture in which worshipers are not told every move to make. In my mind, we want to create a church culture in which worshipers exercise themselves volitionally in engaging with the Lord. The more we direct their responses, the more passive they will become. We don't want to condition people to be passive responders only, but also active initiators who "make His praise glorious" (Ps 66:2). Sometimes a congregation is unusually tired for understandable reasons. For example, if a church is in a series of special meetings each night, by the last night everyone might be more tired than normal. What should a worship leader do when the people are tired? There's not one answer for every situation. Follow the Holy Spirit's lead. There may be times when you will decide to have a spirited time of praise and then progress quickly to other aspects of the meeting. Not every service requires a lengthy worship time.

DEALING WITH RUTS IN WORSHIP

Every church has the natural tendency, over the course of time, to develop ruts in worship. As a church develops its culture and traditions, we find ways to worship that fit comfortably with our church's style. And we stick with it. After a while, it can become a rut.

Somebody once described a rut as a coffin with the ends knocked out. Ruts can be deadly. Smooth, but deadly. Comfortable, but deadly. Predictable, but deadly. When a worship service is smooth, it can mean that God is doing a deep work in His people, but it can also mean we're in a rut. When we default back into our standard worship rut, the Lord is willing to work with us and help us. He doesn't want us to settle for worship services that are so comfortable that we disengage and just coast.

Ruts are usually vacated by doing something uncomfortable, fresh, or out of the ordinary. Sometimes we need to take a step or a jump in a new direction. Be careful to follow the Spirit's lead. To get out of a rut can be a jarring, jolting experience, but afterward there can come a fresh flow and vitality in worship.

Most people naturally resist change. Ruts are familiar, predictable, and comfortable. It can be tempting for worship leaders to back off and just maintain the status quo. But sometimes the Spirit will constrain leaders to press forward into something fresh in Him.

When longing for the fresh movements of the Holy Spirit, sometimes all we can do it wait quietly on the Lord for His direction. Some people don't know what to do with corporate silence. They think it's wrong and needs to be fixed, so they'll just say something or sing something. It's true, corporate silence can feel awkward; however, it can also be profoundly meaningful. It can foster a sense of reverence, awe, careful listening, holy desire, and expectation.

Refusing to cruise smoothly along in our church rut requires courage. One of the most courageous things a worship leader can do is back off from the mic and make room for the Holy Spirit. Have you ever considered inviting the entire room to go to their knees in surrender to God?

Is it possible to come away from a worship service satisfied and pleased while the Lord Jesus wanted so much more for us? Ultimately, the purpose of corporate worship is fulfilled not when the people are pleased but when the Lord is pleased. After all, the worship service was meant for Him all along.

Now, here's the other side of it. While it's occasionally appropriate to do something "out of the box" to escape a worship rut, it's also appropriate at times to avoid sharp directional changes in the service. Holy Spirit-led meetings usually have a smooth flow that is decent and orderly (1 Cor 14:40). In Scripture, the Holy Spirit's movements are likened to wind, water, oil, and fire. When the oil of the Spirit is flowing smoothly and gently, let's partner with Him by avoiding sharp turns and screeching halts.

SETTING GOALS FOR WORSHIP

Consider setting some goals for the corporate worship life of your congregation. Without a progressive vision, we tend to lose forward momentum and become stagnant. Reach for a vision that's larger than just this coming Sunday, but that looks toward the future.

Our vision for worship should be progressive so that,

when stated goals are reached, new goals can be articulated. If our vision for worship was crafted a number of years ago, it's possibly outdated and should be revisited.

I recommend adopting goals for corporate worship that are so clear they are actually written down. People like to follow leaders who can articulate where we're going. Consider writing goals according to the following guidelines.

Make your goals *tangible*. In other words, make them concrete enough that we know when we've reached them. We don't want goals that are abstract, ethereal, or vague. Don't simply aim for "better worship." We all want better worship, but what does that mean? What does it look like? How can it be measured? How can we recognize when we've reached it?

Adopt goals that are *achievable*. If our goals are unrealistic, our team can become discouraged in the journey. Have some short-term goals that produce the delight of quick achievement, and then some long-term goals that give us a sense of vision and purpose.

Translate goals into *action initiatives*. Lay out the steps we plan to take to reach our goals. Might we even want to put dates or deadlines on certain action items?

I'd like to suggest a way for your worship ministry to formulate its goals. Set aside a block of time, perhaps on a Friday night or Saturday, for everyone on the worship ministry to gather. Serve pizza, and then after prayer, have a time of vision casting. Simply ask the team, "What goals should we set for our worship ministry?" You might be amazed at how vibrant the discussion is, because your team is really invested.

Work the goals over until they're clear and concrete. Here are some hypothetical ideas to help give a feel for how your goals could be expressed:

- Have 90% of the congregation actually singing versus just standing and watching.

- Have 25% of our congregation attend occasional evenings of worship in which we focus on the Lord for longer periods of time.

- Develop a system for raising up musicians from our congregation.
- Use Scripture more intentionally to inspire worship.
- Write more songs collaboratively with two or more songwriters in our church.
- Get five more teen musicians functioning on our team within the next year.
- Produce a recording of worship songs written by songwriters within our church family.
- Write a new song for every sermon series our pastor preaches this year.
- Strengthen our church's worship vocabulary in certain specific themes (such as the cross, intimacy, faith, hope, etc.).
- Find ways to make old hymns more meaningful for our church.
- Help our congregation become more spontaneous and self-articulate in worship, rather than being entirely song-dependent.
- Use more songs that focus specifically on Jesus.

Every worship ministry should have a goal of raising up worshipers who worship Jesus as a way of life and not just at corporate gatherings. We're not laboring merely for 20 hot minutes on a Sunday morning; we're laboring to develop disciples who worship Jesus in a 24/7 reality. May the Lord show us how we can inspire believers to love Jesus passionately seven days a week and then bring that fire to our corporate worship services.

While we want to have goals for worship, we also want to delight in the Lord right where we are. We should be at rest simply in enjoying Him in the moment. Let's not become so visionary that we miss today's opportunity to bask in His presence. Yes, we want to be visionary; but we also want to be present in the present. Being with Him, right now, is all we need.

There's a balance here that Paul articulated in the book of Philippians. He spoke of being content in whatever state he was in (Phil 4:11), but then he also spoke of "forgetting those things which are behind and reaching forward to those things which are ahead" (Phil 3:13). So we do *both*. We're content with Jesus in the present, but we reach forward to what He has ahead for us.

This new millennium has seen a mighty wave of worship crescendo throughout the body of Christ. New songs have exploded all over the globe. Entire denominations have been revitalized. The church is singing like never before. New life is springing up everywhere! And the song is only going to increase. Isaiah prophesied about it:

> Behold, the former things have come to pass, and new things I declare; before they spring forth I tell you of them. Sing to the LORD a new song, and His praise from the ends of the earth, you who go down to the sea, and all that is in it, you coastlands and you inhabitants of them! Let the wilderness and its cities lift up their voice, the villages that Kedar inhabits. Let the inhabitants of Sela sing, let them shout from the top of the mountains (Isa 42:9-11).

God's purposes for music and worship in the church are increasing and blossoming. God is imparting His heartbeat to worship leaders and worshipers today so we can participate in His purposes. Where is God taking us in worship in these last days? Actually, I've written a book in answer to that question. Check out the title, *FOLLOWING THE RIVER: A Vision For Corporate Worship*. It articulates where God is taking us in worship in this hour.

May you be part of the expansion of God's kingdom in this momentous hour of history. Jesus is coming soon!

CHAPTER 9

THE WORSHIP TEAM

A phenomenon has erupted on the stage of corporate worship in recent years: Congregational worship is being led today by *teams* of musicians and singers. King David had Levites ministering in teams in his day, but the practice fell into disrepair for centuries and just now has been rediscovered.

Only a few decades ago, most congregational worship was led by one leader who was supported by one or two musicians. Things are radically different today. One person still usually functions as the worship leader but is now surrounded by an entire team that ministers together around a shared purpose.

The goal of the worship team is not simply to worship the Lord themselves, but to give the congregation the best opportunity possible to worship. We're not simply trying to get a bonfire going on the platform; we're seeking to start a forest fire in the congregation. To say it another way, a worship service is not successful until the entire congregation has experienced a release in worship.

The team pioneers the way, and the people follow. Micah portrayed it like this: "The one who breaks open will come up before them; they will break out, pass through the gate, and go out by it; their king will pass before them, with the LORD at their head" (Mic 2:13). In that same spirit, the worship team breaks open a way in music and song so that the congregation can follow.

While some worship ministries call themselves a *worship band*, I will use the term *worship team* in this book. Whatever term you prefer, let's look at how worship teams minister together.

THE BENEFITS OF TEAM MINISTRY

There are two general ways in which a team enhances the effectiveness of worship ministry. First, with a team there's safety and help.

I traveled with a worship team for a few years, conducting services in many churches, and I learned the blessing of having a team for support. To be honest, I don't flow in the fullest anointing of the Spirit 100% of the time. In my weaker moments, I've needed the strengths of the other team members. So many times I thanked God in my heart for those on my worship team because, when I was weak, they would rally and throw in their weight. The first benefit of team ministry, therefore, is support.

Second, a team provides unity, and unity increases spiritual impact. One leader may have a good ministry in worship, but surround that leader with a team of Spirit-filled musicians and the effectiveness of that ministry is multiplied.

The Lord said to the nation of Israel, "Five of you shall chase a hundred, and a hundred of you shall put ten thousand to flight" (Lev 26:8). In other words, unity produces exponential impact. When a vision is communicated clearly, and a team gathers prayerfully around that vision, the kingdom of God advances dynamically in a region.

Many worship teams are comprised of three general classifications: the worship leader, musicians, and singers. Some teams might add classifications for media operators, sound technicians, lighting technicians, dancers, sign language interpreters, banner bearers, etc. Whatever the classifications, all are part of the team.

Let's work from the following diagram in our discussion of the worship team:

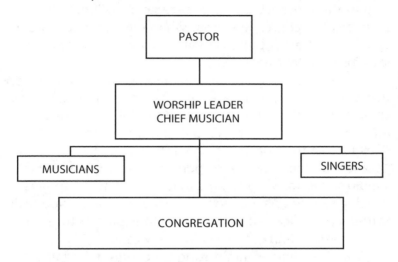

For starters, the pastor's role in worship is the most important in determining the success of the worship ministry. Let's look at it.

THE ROLE OF THE PASTOR

Corporate worship in the local church will likely never exceed the vision and values of the pastor. In most churches, the pastor regulates that church's worship culture. Pastors envision, care for, release, monitor, and support those in worship ministry. No one can mobilize and motivate the worship team more effectively than the pastor. The pastor's worship theology and ministry philosophy are huge factors in shaping and determining the course of the worship ministry.

Pastors should look for strategic ways to interface with the worship team at significant moments. For example, some pastors meet for prayer with the worship team before services. Who better to teach the team how to pray? That can be a great time to communicate about where we hope to go with the meeting.

Pastors are key to the worship ministry in their role as *lead worshiper*. Pastors who demonstrate wholehearted worship in the presence of the congregation will help to birth a worshiping church. It's great when pastors preach about worship, but even better when they exemplify passionate love for Jesus in a visible way.

Pastors hold a place of influence in the congregation that's sobering. To illustrate my meaning, suppose a guest speaker says some things from the pulpit that are on the edge of controversy. What's the first thing the people do? They look at their pastors to read their body language. The people read their pastors' responses to determine how they should respond. Something similar sometimes happens in worship services. As the service is in progress, worshipers will sometimes glance in the direction of their pastors to see how they're responding to the worship service.

A worship leader might exhort a congregation in a certain expression of praise, but if the pastors fail to follow the worship leader's exhortation, most of the people will likewise be slow to follow. And the opposite is also true. If pastors are the first ones to shout for joy before the Lord, others will probably follow their example. In some churches, the pastors' demeanor can do more to influence the participation of the congregation than the efforts of the musicians, singers, and worship leader combined.

The worship service is not the time for pastors to be counting attendees or checking to see who made the service. Nor is it the time to be reviewing the order of service with the pastoral team. It's time to worship the Lord of heaven and earth. What could be more important, in that moment, than ministering to the Lord?

In the book of Revelation, the elders serve as lead worshipers, often falling prostrate before the King in a way that inspires all of heaven to follow their example (Rev 5:8, 14). If elders have known the Lord longer and more deeply than others, then it seems most natural for them to be leading the way in worship. Just as it's fitting for the Lord to be exalted in the council of the elders (Ps 107:32), it's fitting that pastors and elders lead the flock in exalting the name of Jesus.

As the "pastor" of the nation of Israel, King David was the first worshiper among the people. He's a great model for pastors today. He purposely worshiped in the presence of all the people. When the ark was brought to Zion, he donned a linen ephod and danced before the Lord with all his might. Why? Because his affections for his Savior rippled through every fiber of his being.

When despised by his wife, Michal, for his open display of exuberance, he responded, "It was before the LORD, who chose me instead of your father and all his house, to appoint me ruler over the people of the LORD, over Israel. Therefore I will play music before the LORD. And I will be even more undignified than this, and will be humble in my own sight. But as for the maidservants of whom you have spoken, by them I will be held in honor" (2 Sam 6:21-22).

David set aside his pride and devoted himself to exalting the Lord extravagantly. May today's pastors and elders do likewise.

Pastors also fulfill a lead role in determining the level of excellence in a church's music department. One tangible way that's expressed is through the church's budget. Pastors who value musical excellence will ensure that the church allocates sufficient resources to fund the needs of the music department, enabling the music department to grow and flourish.

Also, it goes a long way when pastors express appreciation publicly for the labors of the worship team. Those involved in worship ministry are arguably some of the hardest working laborers in the entire congregation.

Pastors, what is your philosophy of worship? Do you view it as a *song* service or a *worship* service? Are the songs merely *preliminaries* that prepare the people for the sermon? Is music a means to church growth? Is singing sometimes just a time filler—something to do while the offering is being collected? Is a song a way to give people a break after they've been sitting a long time? Is it a signal to the people in the foyer that the service has started and it's time to come in?

I submit that worship is something far grander than any of that. It's the primary reason we come together. We gather to lift high the name of Jesus and minister to Him in the beauty of holiness. We gather to establish the presence of Christ in our city and region. When pastors appreciate the glorious nature of corporate worship, they can infuse that value into the culture of the local church.

THE ROLE OF THE WORSHIP LEADER

Worship teams are configured in all kinds of ways these days. In many churches, the main worship leader is also the leader of the entire worship ministry. But there are exceptions. What follows, therefore, is not an attempt to dictate how a worship ministry should be configured. Rather, our focus is on principles that enable worship leaders to function effectively. Just apply the principles in a way that fits your context.

Worship leaders provides overall leadership for the congregation, musicians, and singers. They are concerned for both the musical and spiritual dynamics of the worship service.

Worship leaders select and start most of the songs to be sung. Spiritual discernment is used to determine what song should be sung, at what time we should progress to the next song, and what the next song should be. One way worship leaders discern what song to sing next is by asking themselves what song they themselves *want* to sing. That's a very simple way the Holy Spirit moves our hearts and helps us choose the next song to sing.

Worship leaders don't move through their set list like an ipod playlist, with one track automatically following another. The songs on the set list are viewed as options or suggestions—a helpful reference as they seek to flow with the movements of the Holy Spirit in the moment.

One way effective worship leaders lead a congregation is by showing them that they themselves are worshipers. When worship leaders step outside the bounds of just being the service leader, and throw their heart and soul into worship, the people gladly follow. People love authenticity on the platform. In fact, this is how everyone on the worship team leads—by showing an authentic love for Jesus with each song that's sung. Sometimes the congregation will see that the musicians are having a good time grooving to the music, and that's okay, but we want them to see more than that. We want them to see prophetic musicians who are engaged spiritually in offering their love to Jesus Christ.

Worship leaders or musicians might get distracted for a moment with the need to address a technical detail (such as a sound loop, or a feedback problem, or instructions for the musicians), but once the specifics have been relayed and understood, they step right back into the spirit of the meeting with all their hearts.

Worship leaders should be intentional about training up new worship leaders, singers, and musicians. New worship leaders can be raised up by having them lead at the side of a seasoned worship leader. Drummers should seek to reproduce themselves in other drummers; singers should work to raise up other singers; worship leaders should mentor other worship leaders. This principle applies to the whole team. Everyone on the worship team should strive to reproduce themselves in others.

How can we bring new team members up to speed? Start by training them in the rehearsal time, and then let them intern in actual worship services. During a service, you may have them stand next to a team member and learn at their side. Tailor the training process uniquely to each individual. We want them to grow in musical proficiency, learn how to function on a team, and become someone who inspires others by the way they worship.

After services, consider debriefing with the team. Everyone can learn from what just happened. With helpful input and feedback to those being trained, a worship team becomes a spiritual greenhouse for new team members to grow, mature, and thrive.

Worship leaders, use team rehearsals as an opportunity to impart vision. Let the grace that rests on your life become contagious. Ask for help to impart passion and vision to every person on the team.

THE PASTOR/WORSHIP LEADER RELATIONSHIP

The pastor/worship leader relationship has the potential to be one of the most powerful partnerships in the life of the local church. I see a biblical template for their relationship in Psalm 149:6, "Let the high praises of God be in their mouth, and a two-edged sword in their hand." Explosive synergy can be found when the ministry of high praises (the worship leader) links up with the ministry of the two-edged word of God (the teaching role of the pastor).

Rather than vying for platform time, these two cooperate and labor together for the edification of the congregation. They celebrate the unique gifts each one has and delight in the joy of running together in ministry. They help each other be even more effective in their calling. After all, they lean on each other really hard. A pastor needs a strong, anointed worship leader; a worship leader needs a capable, anointed preacher.

When the two come together, something explosive happens. A praising church without a strong ministry in the word will flap around in circles like a one-winged bird; but a praising church with a strong pulpit ministry will thrive. When oxygen unites with gas, watch out for combustion!

Three ingredients help maintain a healthy relationship between the pastor and worship leader: *respect, consideration*, and *communication*.

1. Respect one another

We respect each other's integrity, calling, gifts, sincerity, wisdom, and expertise. Respect means the worship leader stays inside the time limit allotted in a service. And respect means that, if the worship leader goes longer, the pastor assumes there was a compelling reason in the Holy Spirit. Respect means that the pastor gives the worship leader room to follow their heart and instincts. Respect means that the worship leader sees to it the entire team sits in on the sermon. Respect means we give each other space to make a mistake. And it means we don't try to fulfill the other's function.

2. Be considerate

We become considerate of each other when we care about the other's concerns more than our own. As Paul wrote, "Let each of you look out not only for his own interests, but also for the interests of others" (Phil 2:4). Worship leaders should consider that pastors have much more on their radar than just the time of singing; pastors should consider that worship leaders have invested *hours* of preparation for the worship service. Worship leaders should consider that pastors can sometimes be matter-of-fact; pastors should consider that worship leaders can sometimes be emotionally vulnerable.

How considerate we are of each other can be tested at times when there are differences of opinion—for example, on what should happen next in a worship service. The worship leader might think it's time to move to the next song, and the pastor might feel like we need to sing the previous song again. When there's a difference of opinion, which one has the mind of the Lord? In such instances, we could probably go either option and move with God's Spirit. The question isn't whose discernment is right; the question is, are we considerate of each other in those moments of decision?

You'll recall that Amos said, "A lion has roared! Who will not fear? The Lord GOD has spoken! Who can but prophesy?" (Amos 3:8). In other words, when God is speaking, almost *everybody* could feel inspired to prophesy. A similar dynamic can happen in corporate worship. When the Spirit of God is moving in a worship service, almost *everyone* on the leadership team can see a great direction to take. When both pastor and worship leader are aware the Holy Spirit is working dynamically, and both feel inspired by the Spirit but in different directions, they must be considerate of each other.

One way pastors can be considerate of worship leaders is by deferring to them, even when the pastors know they could provide more capable leadership in that moment. And one way worship leaders can be considerate of pastors is by delighting in their expertise to lead the people into powerful encounters with God.

3. Communicate consistently

Amos asked, "Can two walk together, unless they are agreed?" (Amos 3:3). Walking together in agreement requires communication. If the pastor and worship leader don't interact sufficiently, the partnership is likely to fray and deteriorate.

The first thing to talk through is their philosophy of worship ministry. What are our values and objectives in corporate worship? How important is worship in the life of our particular congregation? How much time will be given to worship in our services? Agreement here is absolutely essential.

Pastors can help worship leaders tune into the church's culture and platform style. When worship leaders know the ropes, and why they're in place, they can cheerfully stay inside them.

This relationship is vitally important to the health of a local church, and the adversary knows it. Therefore, the relationship is vulnerable and often targeted by the enemy in ways that can produce frustration, misunderstanding, annoyance, exasperation, disappointment, wrong assumptions, and even offense. A pastor can be disturbed by a worship leader's apparent insensitivity to the Spirit's movements; a worship leader may be frustrated by a pastor's expectations; a pastor can assume a worship leader isn't committed enough; a worship leader can assume the pastor doesn't value them; a pastor can be frustrated with a worship leader's resistance to constructive feedback; a worship leader can feel like the pastor is intimidating; a pastor can feel like a worship leader is not fully submitted; a worship leader can feel like the pastor doesn't trust their discernment.

Feelings such as these can produce a breach in the partnership if not brought into the light, talked about, and worked through.

Here's an actual example. A pastor got up in the middle of a worship service, grabbed a mic, and spontaneously took the meeting in a direction that was totally different from what the worship leader was expecting. The next day, the worship leader sat down and asked, "Did you feel like you had to save the service from my incompetence?" At that, the pastor just laughed and said, "Just the opposite! You were doing such a fantastic job that the Spirit of God fell on me, and I couldn't help myself!" The accuser didn't want them to talk, but wanted offense to drive a wedge between them. Communication disarmed what could have become a root of bitterness, and turned it into an occasion for encouragement and affirmation.

When you encounter a difference, one way to express yourself is to say something like, "I know you didn't mean to do this, but when you made that change in the service, here's how it made me feel." This kind of approach is honest without being accusatory.

So many powerful ministry partnerships have been splintered by the adversary because the two didn't talk. Worship leaders sometimes harbor frustrations until they reach a breaking point and leave the church. Many pastors have been caught by surprise, totally unaware that a breach had been simmering for a long time. Communication is so important!

A pastor can lead the way by establishing rules in the relationship that make it safe to be honest and vulnerable. Furthermore, wise pastors will occasionally ask questions such as, "How do you feel about our working relationship?"

"Have you been enjoying leading the services?" "Do you like the direction our services have been going?" "Are you fulfilled in your ministry?"

Communication will help a pastor and worship leader grow in their appreciation for each other. They'll come to depend more and more on the other's strengths. If the lines of communication are open, a quick glance at the pastor can say, "I really don't know what to do next...got any ideas?" And similarly, rather than taking the microphone from the hand of a struggling worship leader, the pastor can reassuringly whisper, "I'm here to help if you need me."

Communicate appreciation for one another—both privately and publicly. It's almost impossible to express too much appreciation and thanksgiving for each other. Say it over and over, "I'm so thankful to God for you!"

In my opinion, pastors should not be too restrictive in what they allow worship leaders to do. Some worship leaders are permitted to do nothing but lead songs, but that can become frustrating in its limitations. I say this because leading worship is actually a pastoral function. Worship leaders guide the flock to green pastures and still waters. In a worship service, a congregation is actually going somewhere together. Worship leaders have a pastoral heart to help the flock get there, and sometimes songs are not everything the journey needs. Powerful things can happen in corporate worship when worship leaders have the freedom to do such things as pray, read Scripture, offer an exhortation, take the offering, lead in Communion, pray for the sick, or invite the people to respond to a specific leading of the Holy Spirit such as a call to repentance. Each church must establish its own guidelines for what a worship leader is permitted to do. I'm advocating for generosity and freedom in the Holy Spirit.

I have one final thing to say to worship leaders regarding their relationship with their pastor: Never become a sounding board for those who are discontent with the pastor. If someone comes to you with a grievance against the pastor, don't let them find a sympathetic ear. Rather, tell them they must make an appointment with the pastor (in the spirit of Matthew 18:15). Always preserve your loyal spirit.

THE ROLE OF THE CHIEF MUSICIAN

Let me explain why I'm using the term, *chief musician*. It was commonly used in David's day, seen in the titles of fifty-five psalms. For example, in the title to Psalm 4 it says, "To the Chief Musician. With stringed instruments. A Psalm of David" (Ps 4:0). In David's time, new songs were given to the Chief Musician so they could be incorporated into the worship vocabulary of the nation.

What do I mean when I use the term? For me, the chief musician is the person on the worship team who provides primary musical leadership to all the team's musicians. You could use another workable designation such as *the band leader*. The title chosen is not so important; what's important is that your worship team know which person on the team provides bottom-line leadership to the musicians. Somebody needs to have the final musical word.

This role is strategically important and should be assigned very prayerfully. The chief musician should have the respect of the team because of their musical prowess and ability to build teamwork. Among their duties, they will probably choose or create musical arrangements, decide how chord sheets will be notated, rehearse music with the musicians, and orchestrate the musicians in a way that helps each one know their place in each song.

On some teams, the worship leader and chief musician are the same person. But not always, because not all worship leaders are strong musicians on an instrument.

In cases where the worship leader and chief musician are two different people, the worship team can still function very effectively. Let me mention a couple things to keep in mind.

First of all, in most cases the chief musician serves in a supportive capacity under the leadership of the worship leader.

The chief musician is usually empowered to make final musical decisions—such as which chords are to be played, which harmonies are to be sung, the role each instrument should take, etc. Wise worship leaders will maximize the chief musician's gifts by releasing them to function freely. Where chief musicians are released to exercise their craft, the excellence of the ministry will grow and the grace on the team will increase.

Look back at what we said earlier in this chapter about the pastor/worship leader relationship. The principles guiding that relationship (*respect, consideration,* and *communication*) should also guide the worship leader/chief musician relationship.

Every church needs a strong chief musician. What should a smaller church do that has no chief musician in the midst? Pray! Even better, watch and pray. What I mean is, *pray* for God to send a chief musician, and then *watch* for when that person shows up. I've also known of smaller churches contacting larger churches nearby and finding a qualified musician who was willing to come over and help.

THE ROLE OF THE MUSICIANS

Musicians are more than *accompanists* to singing. They are Spirit-empowered minstrels who are impregnated with a holy mandate to lead God's people in worship. They inspire, break open, support, and prophesy on their instruments.

David approached the ministry of music in the Lord's tabernacle very soberly, as seen here:

> Then David spoke to the leaders of the Levites to appoint their brethren to be the singers accompanied by instruments of music, stringed instruments, harps, and cymbals, by raising the voice with resounding joy (1 Chron 15:16).

> And with them Heman and Jeduthun and the rest who were chosen, who were designated by name,

to give thanks to the LORD, because His mercy endures forever; and with them Heman and Jeduthun,
to sound aloud with trumpets and cymbals and the
musical instruments of God (1 Chron 16:41-42).

In the Scriptures that describe how musicians were
placed in David's tabernacle, you'll encounter words such as
appoint, responsible, designated, and *chosen.* The musicians
weren't just slapped together quickly from a pool of volun-
teers; rather, they were appointed and consecrated to their
post because they qualified to minister to the Lord.

We should approach the ministry of worship in the local
church with similar sobriety. Being a capable musician is not
the only requirement. We look beyond the art and consider the heart. Musicians should be true worshipers who are
called of the Lord and appointed by church leaders.

Musicians are *initiators* of worship. Therefore, we're looking for them to meet some basic qualifications. Even if these
qualifications aren't in full bloom yet, we want musicians
who are sincerely reaching toward the following:

1. Worshipers first

We want those who are worshipers first, musicians second. Said another way, we want them to have the first commandment in first place. We want them to be in love with
Jesus and devoted to expressing that love. They should
demonstrate they're worshipers whether on the platform or
off, whether in the midst of the congregation or someplace
where no one's watching.

2. Worshiper on the instrument

Secondly, we want musicians who love to worship the
Lord on their instrument. They don't simply *play* their instrument; they *worship* on their instrument. They don't just jam;
they prophesy. They're not simply into music; they're into
Jesus. We're looking for musicians who worship the Lord

on their instrument when they're home alone. Let's not be tempted to bring sizzling musicians onto the platform who raise the team's bar of musical proficiency but, because of their compromising lifestyle, dilute the spiritual effectiveness of the worship ministry.

Some churches hire unbelievers to serve as musicians during worship because they don't have believing musicians in the congregation. If an unbelieving musician is your only option, I suggest you pray persistently for the Spirit to apprehend them in the middle of a service and draw them to believing faith. Until they're awakened to love for Christ, their ability to lead the congregation will be limited.

We want the preacher of the word to be a believer in Jesus who can inspire the saints through their knowledge of Christ; why not also ask God for believing musicians who are called to lead God's people in praise and worship?

3. Disciple of Jesus

A musician should model a consistent Christian walk. Musicians hold a prominent place in our assemblies, and the young people in the church look to them as role models and examples. We want role models on our platforms who will inspire young people to be devout followers of Jesus.

4. Call

Musicians should be *appointed* to the team. They should believe they're called of God to lead others in worship, and that calling should be affirmed by the church leadership in accordance with the Spirit's witness.

5. Commitment

We want musicians who feel the Lord has joined them to our local church, at least for this season. They should care sincerely for the health and increase of this community of believers.

6. Musicianship

And finally, church musicians should meet a church's standards of musical proficiency. In David's time, musicians were appointed who were *instructed* and *skillful* (1 Chron 25:7). Yes, we want the heart; but we also need musicians who have mastered the art.

Many churches have asked whether they should allow believing musicians to join their worship team who also play in secular contexts such as nightclubs. I'm not sure there's one blanket answer that fits all. I've known church musicians who have felt called to consecrate their musical gifts to the Lord alone, and who refuse on principle to prostitute that gifting in a worldly context. In accordance with 2 Chronicles 7:6 and 30:21, they view their instrument as exclusively the Lord's. But I've known other worshiping musicians who have felt a divine call to take their musicianship to places where unbelievers gather and be salt and light in dark places. The answer to this question, therefore, lies with each instance, and is found by seeking the mind of the Spirit (Rom 8:14).

THE ROLE OF THE SINGERS

Singers serve to support the worship leader and help to lead the congregation in singing. They reinforce the melody and also sing harmonies that make the sound of the song more pleasant. Usually they use a microphone to be more effective in this role.

We amplify their voices not to drown out but to draw out the congregation.

When we consider qualifications for singers on the worship team, we want them to meet some of the musicians' qualifications listed above, namely:

1. **Followers of Jesus**
2. **Worshipers first**
3. **Called**

4. Committed

In addition, let me add a couple other qualifications for singers:

5. Vocal abilities

Singers should be able to pass a worship team's entrance audition. An audition evaluates vocal control, pitch control, music hearing abilities, the skill to harmonize, vocal range, and the ability to carry a melody in a way others can easily follow.

6. Liberty

Singers should have the confidence to freely express body language in worship. In other words, they should have no reservations or inhibitions about biblical expressions such as lifting their hands, dancing, kneeling, clapping, shouting, bowing, weeping, etc.

7. Contagion

We want singers who have a contagious love for Jesus. Their countenances should reflect delight in the Lord's presence and a fixation upon the face of Christ. One of their primary functions on the platform is to inspire the congregation to join them. People are often led more strongly by what they *see* than what they *hear*. It's not helpful if the singers facing the congregation look like they're in pain while worshiping. We want to cultivate a countenance that inspires, not distracts. With personal coaching, even someone who naturally scowls can learn to adopt a pleasing persona when standing before the people.

Some folk smile and shine almost effortlessly while worshiping the Lord. They're great to have on your worship team! I consider their ability to radiate the joy and peace of Christ even more valuable than their vocal abilities.

What should you do if you have someone on the team who isn't a very good singer but is highly contagious and inspirational as a worshiper? Here's my take on it. Give them a microphone—and turn it off. Even if they can't stay on pitch, they can inspire the congregation to open to the Lord.

In addition to a select group of singers with microphones, some churches have a *worshiping choir* that sings on the platform but doesn't hold microphones. For churches that choose this option, I see three potential benefits. First, this means they have even more zealous worshipers on the platform inspiring a spirit of worship in the congregation. Second, it makes participation on the team attainable to more people, giving the participants greater joy and ownership in the body. And third, it means the audition leader doesn't have to say *no* as often to eager applicants. Those who don't qualify as singers may qualify for the larger choir.

SOUND, MEDIA, AND SCREENS

Sound system operators are part of the worship team. They're central, not peripheral, to this ministry. They run sound for worship team rehearsals and get all the sound settings ready for the corporate gathering. When they join team rehearsals, a sense of solidarity is fostered with the team. Those on the platform couldn't do it without the sound technicians.

Sound techs are on high alert throughout a worship service. They keep their eyes riveted on the platform so they don't miss anything. If someone reaches for a mic that's not on, they notice and immediately turn it on. If a musician is trying to signal a desire to them, they catch it right away and make the necessary adjustments. Worship leaders *love* an attentive sound operator who catches their signals immediately and adjusts accordingly.

Leaders find ways to affirm and thank sound board operators publicly and privately for their powerful role in the worship ministry. To the casual observer, they really don't do much except stand behind a console of controls. But to those in the know, they work very hard to enable corporate worship.

Media and screen operators are also important members of the worship team. Some teams don't expect the screen operator—the person who selects the song lyrics for the screens—to be present for worship team rehearsals. But, in my opinion, their presence is really helpful. Why? Because the projecting of lyrics on the screens during worship is a vitally important element in congregational worship. When the screen operator is not fully familiar with the song, they can make a number of mistakes. They can project the lyrics too late; they can put up the wrong lyrics; they can hit the wrong frame and miss the nuances of a couple missing words. With each mistake, the people are distracted and the spirit of worship in the congregation is compromised. If the media operators come to the team rehearsal and project the lyrics during rehearsal, they master each song in rehearsal and then are able to serve the congregation seamlessly.

Screen operators should have musical abilities because it takes a musical ear to follow a song and know which frame to select next. The operator should be able to sing every song on the set list, just like the singers on the team. When the worship leader gets creative and goes to a verse or bridge out of sequence, a sharp operator recognizes the change instantaneously and compensates with lightning speed. Yes, musical skills are very important to this role.

Here's the thing about media and sound operators. When they're doing their job competently, nobody notices. But when they make a mistake, *everybody* notices. Their role on the worship team, therefore, is so very highly valued.

WHEN TO WATCH FOR SIGNALS

Many worship teams use a talkback microphone system to communicate among team members. Here's how a talkback mic works. The worship leader can hit a foot pedal switch that activates the talkback function on their mic. With the switch engaged, the worship leader can talk on the microphone and their voice goes exclusively to the headsets of the team members. Nobody in the congregation can hear what they're saying. So they can say something like, "Stop the click track, let's slow down, and then move into the next song." When they disengage the talkback function with the foot switch, they can resume singing the song over the room's sound system.

Talkback microphones are a brilliant way for worship teams to communicate. Anyone who needs one can have one—whether the sound operator, worship leader, chief musician, etc. This makes the communication of directives to the musicians and singers and sound techs, in the middle of a worship service, easier than ever. I bet David could have wished he had access to this kind of equipment in his tabernacle at Zion. Sometimes technology is a beautiful thing.

Churches that don't have this technology will want to develop a set of hand signals to communicate with the team while worship is in progress. For hand signals to work there must be ongoing *visual contact* among team members. Eye contact between team members is especially critical at the following points of *each song*:

1. At the start

2. At transition points in the song

When you're at the end of a chorus or bridge or verse, watch for any signals. The worship leader may want to pause and say something, or repeat a line in a way that wasn't planned.

3. Frequently throughout

Have you ever noticed a worship leader trying to communicate something to a certain musician or singer, but they can't get their attention? It's frustrating to the leader and distracting to everyone who notices. Musicians, do your leader a favor and look over at them repeatedly during a song.

4. At the end

The worship leader may want to repeat the song, move

directly into another song, change keys, stop singing altogether, or incorporate a slow finish. Visual contact with the worship leader is critical at the end of a song so the entire team can stay in sync together.

KINDS OF SIGNALS TO USE

Each worship team should develop its own set of *team signals* to communicate with each other in the middle of a worship service. Most signals used by worship teams are hand signals, but some leaders will also raise the neck of their guitar or find some other creative means of signaling.

The actual signals chosen will vary with each worship team, but the meanings of the signals are commonly along these lines:

1. The song's key

For example, two fingers pointed up could mean the key of 2 sharps, and two fingers pointed down could mean the key of 2 flats. If a leader wants to do a song that wasn't planned, a signal to a musician could indicate, "Give me a D chord." Then the worship leader could launch into the new song.

2. Raise the key (a thumbs up could suffice)

3. Change the volume

A palm motion up or down, for example, could communicate the desire to be louder or softer.

4. The chords in a song

If an unplanned song is suddenly started and the musicians don't know its chords, hand signals can communicate the chords of the song. For example, three fingers could indicate a three chord, five fingers indicate the five chord, etc.

5. Voices only

It's helpful to have a signal that tells all the musicians to stop playing, so the song can be sung with voices only, or voices and drums only.

6. Repeat

Devise a signal that tells everyone on the team you want to repeat what was just sung or played.

7. Go to the chorus

8. Change of tempo

You'll want two signals here—one that means speed up, the other that means slow down.

9. Come to a stop (end the song)

TEAM EXPECTATIONS

A worship team should have a list of expectations for every person on the worship team. A paper copy could be given to anyone auditioning for the worship team. There will be general expectations for everyone on the team, and then perhaps more specific requirements for certain positions on the team.

To help you draft a list of team expectations, let me suggest some items you may want to include on your list.

1. A sense of divine call
2. Pastoral affirmation of the appointment
3. Church attendance
4. Lifestyle of worship
5. Spiritual disciplines (prayer, Scripture reading)
6. Spiritual stability
7. Financial stewardship

8. Blamelessness in integrity

9. Team rehearsal attendance

10. Obedience to leader instructions

11. Open to correction

12. Prompt in attendance

13. Personal musical rehearsal

14. Dress code standards

15. Participation in pre-service prayer

Let me add a comment about number eleven, being *open to correction*. Help musicians understand this item before they join the team because it's easy for musicians to take correction more personally than they need to. Here's what I mean. Musicians sometimes view their musical style as an extension of their personality and, if you critique their musical style, they can take it as a personal jab. So it's good to talk about this dynamic even before we start working together. We refuse to become offended when we're asked to adjust our playing. Sometimes we'll need to relinquish the flare of our musical preferences for the sake of the team. If we can do so graciously, there will be other times when our flare will be precisely what is needed and celebrated.

Corporate worship services are not a time for musicians to show off their improvisational abilities or polished skills. Rather, we harness our abilities and channel them into prophetic musicianship—using our musical gifts and spiritual sensitivities to support a release of worship in the congregation.

TEAM REHEARSAL

Worship team rehearsal is essential to the success of the ministry and, since worship happens weekly, rehearsing for it should also happen on a weekly basis. Rehearsal makes us one—both in music and in heart.

If possible, I advise a worship team rehearse on a day other than Sunday. All that's needed on Sunday morning, then, is a relatively brief sound check. This frees up the rest of the pre-service time for prayer.

Again, worship team rehearsal is more than just a musical event. A typical rehearsal, therefore, would probably include some of the following elements:

1. Praise and worship

It's what we do. Since this is our ministry, why not spend time together worshiping? As the team ministers together to the Lord, they'll develop authenticity and unity of purpose—the kind of unity that produces power and effective spiritual service.

2. Teach and study

Use small portions of your weekly rehearsal to teach and discuss biblical truths related to worship. Study the Scriptures together. Read meaningful books on worship as a team and discuss them. I also encourage worship teams to attend a worship conference every year or two, to keep the vision fresh and stay in tune with what God is doing across the body of Christ.

3. Share

Make time for team members to express their hearts and interests. Do life together. Debrief on worship services, and discuss the health of the worship ministry. Cast vision together.

4. Pray

Pray for the concerns each one on the team is carrying. Pray for the congregation and for upcoming services. Make your worship team a praying team. May a spirit of intercession rest upon all that we do.

5. Practice

I've placed musical rehearsal last, but make no mistake, it's very important. At the dedication of Solomon's temple, we're told "the trumpeters and singers were as one, to make one sound to be heard in praising and thanking the LORD" (2 Chron 5:13). This oneness of sound can align only through practice.

The worship team at the dedication of Solomon's temple was rather large. There were 120 trumpeters alone, not to mention the other musicians, as well as a mass choir. They were rehearsed and ready to make *one sound* in praise to the Lord, and when they did, the record declares that, "the house of the LORD was filled with a cloud, so that the priests could not continue ministering because of the cloud; for the glory of the LORD filled the house of God" (2 Chron 5:13-14). God responded in glory to their unity.

How did they come to such unity? They practiced!

Solomon wanted this august occasion marked by pomp, regalia, organization, and precision. So everything was well rehearsed in advance. When the glory of God appeared, they reaped the fruit of their dedicated rehearsal. Isn't it encouraging to see how God responded to their order, organization, and planning? He delights when we take the worship ministry this seriously.

I encourage worship teams to pray together before a service starts. Practice will unify a team musically, but prayer will unify a team spiritually. There are no limits to what you can pray for—team members, the congregation, the worship time, the preacher, visitors, the parking lot attendants, the greeters, the children's ministry, etc.

Now let's talk about planning and preparing for corporate worship.

CHAPTER 10

PLANNING
THE WORSHIP SERVICE

Corporate worship requires preparation and planning. Just as pastors spend hours each week in sermon preparation, worship leaders should invest time in planning for the worship service.

Here's why preparation is so important. When Paul described the believer's spiritual armor, he said our feet are shod "with the preparation of the gospel of peace" (Eph 6:15). Our feet aren't shod with peace; our feet are shod with preparation. If we go into a worship service with no set list and no rehearsal behind us, it's like going to war without shoes. Preparation is as essential to corporate worship as shoes are to a soldier's equipment.

When we fail to plan properly for worship, services tend to lack direction. Planning helps give a meeting focus and purpose. Corporate worship is like a journey—we're trying to go somewhere together. Planning enables us to go together into some place in the heart of God.

Granted, there's a tension between preparation and spontaneity. But even for churches that place a high value on spontaneity in worship, preparation is essential. Preparation actually empowers spontaneity. Preparation gives you confidence to be spontaneous in the moment because you know you have a set list to come back to.

Preparation need not produce inflexibility. Even when we're fully prepared for worship, we need not feel overly bound to our preparation but can still flow with unexpected changes in a service. You can't predict the unexpected. For example, I was well prepared on one occasion to lead worship for a certain service but, when I got to the meeting, I discovered the pastor wanted to take the meeting in a totally different direction. It was challenging, but I laid aside my preparation and flowed creatively with the pastor's desires.

Prepare, but then be ready to follow the Holy Spirit's leadership. Even when we're fully prepared, we still want to listen carefully for the Spirit's voice and lean on His help as the service unfolds. Corporate worship is not successful just because we've finished our set list, but because we've discovered the Lord's heart for our time together. Romance can't be approached in an orchestrated, mechanical way. Love always has an element of spontaneity to it.

Wise worship leaders, therefore, balance the tension between strong preparation and Holy Spirit sensitivity.

NAVIGATE UNCERTAINTY

When planning for worship, sometimes clarity comes quickly and easily. *Praise God!* But at other times, worship leaders struggle to gain clarity on the direction to take. Time spent in prayer doesn't always help. If you've experienced this, you're not alone—this is commonly experienced by worship leaders everywhere. No matter how hard you pray and prepare, things can sometimes remain foggy.

We tend to become introspective in those moments, wondering what's wrong with us. If the Lord reveals a shortcoming in you, then repent. But often the issue isn't a shortcoming in our lives. Usually something is happening in the spirit realm that we can't see. When factors are at work that we don't see, God doesn't want us feeling confident about our preparation. If we're confident, we'll plow forward and miss God. Sometimes, He'll intentionally make us hesitant and uncertain because He wants us leaning extra hard on Him.

There have been times, in leading worship, when I've felt like I was on the back of my heels, with my arms flailing to find balance, and I didn't know whether to fall back or lean forward. Have you ever experienced that feeling? I think God sometimes puts us back on our heels, allowing us to feel off-balance and uncertain so we can be moved more easily by a gentle breath from His Spirit. Uncertainty rivets our eyes on Him. Sometimes He'll even design a worship service to be a disaster so we return to complete dependence upon Him.

If you're overly threatened by uncertainty, then worship leading may not be the vocation for you, smile. But if you can bear the uncertainty, the Lord will train you to become a better follower of His Spirit.

PERSONAL PREPARATION

Worship leaders don't only prepare a set list for the meeting but they also prepare themselves. Preparing a set list is pretty straightforward, but preparing yourself can be much more challenging.

How do we prepare ourselves to lead? By spending time in worship, prayer, and the word. When praying in the Spirit in the secret place, a leader is pursuing sensitivity to the Holy Spirit. We express our longing for a greater anointing of the Spirit upon our life and ministry—just as God anointed Jesus with the Holy Spirit and power (Acts 10:38). In the secret place, we spend time ministering to the Lord, which is our first and highest calling. Our ministry to the Lord before His throne in private then spills over into how we minister in public.

If someone spends thirty minutes in song selection and then only five minutes in prayer asking God to bless the list, they have something to learn about self preparation.

Self preparation is a more rigorous prospect than song preparation. For starters, it takes more time. Song selection might take thirty minutes but personal preparation is a 24/7 reality. We constantly cultivate our hearts by living a life of worship. We covet a level of spiritual sensitivity that comes only through a disciplined, daily, intimate walk with Jesus. Without Him we can do nothing.

When our hearts have crusted over because of the cares of life, we don't wait till the worship service to labor for a personal breakthrough in worship. We press into that breakthrough beforehand, so that by the time the service starts we're free in our hearts to lead and follow the Holy Spirit. This is why we prayerfully guard our hearts during the 24 hours prior to a meeting. We want to bring to the meeting a heart that's already connected to the Lord in worship and affection.

Furthermore, avoid *hurrying* before the service. In other words, do your utmost to avoid having to rush around in order to get to the platform on time. Sometimes something happens unexpectedly that's beyond your control, and you arrive to the meeting stressed out and sweaty. Everyone has their turn at those kinds of surprises. But let's do our best to allow room in our schedule for unplanned delays so that they don't unsettle us. The enemy would be delighted if he could distract us in a way that causes us to lead the meeting with frayed emotions. Be willing to say no to activities that could potentially distract in order to preserve your focus for the meeting. Arrive early to the building so you can quiet your heart before the Lord. The dignity and significance of our calling deserves this kind of attentiveness.

GOD USES HUMAN LEADERSHIP

God chooses *people*. He uses weak, broken leaders. If God has called you to lead worship, be assured that He'll help and enable you to fulfill that calling.

We're all prone to feelings of inadequacy from time to time. Our thoughts can distract us, *"Was that song idea my own carnal thought, or was that really prompted by the Holy Spirit?" "Am I really being led by the Spirit right now, or is this my own natural thinking?"* Don't allow such thoughts to disturb or distract you during the worship service. You've spent time preparing your heart through prayer, so when you have an impulse to go a certain direction in a service, accept by faith that it's from God and step forward with confidence in Him. Later, if you realize that wasn't inspired by God, then ponder the situation and learn from it. But in the immediacy of the moment, move forward in faith, knowing that the Lord honors human leaders and directs their hearts.

God honors human leadership to such an extent that we can make a blunder and He'll still honor the sincerity of our efforts. God doesn't embarrass His leaders publicly just because they led in the wrong song. If we need to be corrected, that should be done privately at a later time with the right leaders, not in the middle of the worship service. So worship leaders can relax. Corporate worship is a safe place for young leaders to grow and learn in the Spirit.

IS THE SET LIST SACRED?

Is there one perfect set list for each worship service? In other words, if we really had the mind of Christ, would there be only one combination of songs that would be right for a given meeting? In my opinion, probably not.

It would be interesting to conduct the following experiment. Suppose we were to ask five excellent, experienced worship leaders to fast and pray regarding an upcoming service, and then have them produce a list of songs they feel inspired to lead by the Holy Spirit. My guess is that they would produce five different set lists, with different songs, and a different theme with each list. And I would also guess that any of the five lists and themes could be used for the service and it would work. Why? Because God is not so concerned about what songs we sing or the order in which we sing them; He wants our *hearts*, regardless of the songs that are sung.

I can imagine a worship leader crying to the Lord, "Oh God, what songs should we sing this Sunday? Should we start with Song A, or Song B? Please, please, show me Your will!" And I can imagine the Lord answering something like,

"I don't really care *what* song you use. Whatever song you choose to open with, give Me your hearts. I want you to rejoice that you're together and that you're with Me. Let's enjoy one another!"

Whether we sing one or twenty songs, He wants our wholehearted affections.

Some worship leaders have the mistaken idea that the solution to any problem in worship is the right song. So if the worship service isn't finding momentum, they'll move to another song. And then another. Routinely singing one song after another doesn't necessarily make for a vibrant worship service. Sometimes the last thing we need is another song. Sometimes, instead of automatically going to the next song on the set list, we need to pause and seek what will open the congregation to the Spirit's way.

Our set list isn't something sacred that we dare not violate; rather, it's a resource of possibilities. The songs are tools designed to help us connect with God's heart. Usually the songs we've prepared will take us there. But if, in that journey to God's heart, a different direction emerges or a different song comes to mind, you're free to go with it. Again, the list isn't sacred.

On the other hand, moving away from the set list doesn't necessarily guarantee a more powerful worship service. Our goal isn't either to stay with or deviate from the list, but to encounter Jesus.

PREPARING A SET LIST

A worship leader should prepare a set list for every corporate worship service. A set list is not constrictive but liberating. How? It liberates us from worrying about what the next song should be. It liberates everyone on the worship team to worship freely because we know where we're going.

In my book *FOLLOWING THE RIVER: A Vision For Corporate Worship*, I liken a set list to a boat. When navigating the waters of the Spirit in corporate worship, a worship leader should come to the meeting prepared with a set list—a boat. But there are times in worship when the Spirit seems to beckon us to get out of the boat and walk on water—that is, to deviate from our prepared list and move into an expression of worship we hadn't prepared. When you have a boat, you gain the courage to get out of the boat. Why? Because if you start to sink, you have a boat you can swim back to. Here's what I mean. If you try to follow the Holy Spirit's lead and go with a song you haven't prepared, and then the service starts to diminish in energy and momentum, you always have a list you can go back to. Be prepared, therefore, with a list and also be ready to become spontaneous in response to the Holy Spirit's lead.

I recommend that worship leaders maintain a Master List of all the songs that are current in their team's repertoire. Outdated songs can be deleted at the right time, and new songs added as they're learned. When planning a set list (a song list for the service), this Master List is the worship leader's friend.

A Master List can be organized according to:

• alphabetical order

• key

• tempo (whether fast or slow)

• theme

• whether new or old

• historic anthems

Songs in the same key and tempo can be grouped together because often it's easy to move between them.

A leader will usually craft a set list by reviewing the Master List. The process of honing the set list will not be identical every time, but let me suggest some elements that could be part of your preparation process.

Start with prayer. Proverbs 21:1 says, "The king's heart is in the hand of the LORD, like the rivers of water; He turns it wherever He wishes." In the spirit of that verse, you might pray, "Lord, as I choose songs for worship, turn my heart toward the songs I should consider first." Then, as you scan the Master List, expect the Lord to stir interest in your heart when your eyes come to the right songs. When you find your own heart interested in singing a certain song, put it on your list.

Your first draft may have more songs than you need, and your next step will be to cull the list down to the right number of songs. After that, you'll arrange them in the right order.

At other times, the songs that strike you might not be enough to fill the entire set, and you'll need to review the Master List a second time to fill in around the skeleton of songs before you. Look at the key, tempo, and theme of the songs you've already chosen, and see if you can find other songs that share similar elements.

When compiling a set list, string songs together based upon theme and mood. To identify the theme of a song, look at its lyric content; to identify the mood of a song, examine its tempo and rhythmic strength (whether smooth and fluid or militant and forceful). Place the songs in your list in an order that provides for smooth transitions between tempos and keys and also provides for a progression in the set. In corporate worship, we're not just singing a bunch of songs thrown together, but we are on a corporate journey. We're going somewhere. Plan a set list that foresees a progression in the Spirit.

Be strategic in planning how you'll introduce new songs to your congregation, and then how you'll reinforce them in subsequent weeks so they're learned by everyone.

Once a set list for the service has been compiled, get a copy to everyone who needs one, such as all team members, media operators, the pastoral team, etc.

How many songs should we have on our set list? Perhaps a couple more than we'll actually need. For example, if you think you'll have time to sing four songs, make a list of four songs, and then maybe one or two backup songs. Having a few more songs in front of you than you'll actually need may give you flexibility of movement as the service progresses.

Switching from one key to another is sometimes a bumpy transition, which is why some leaders keep key changes to a minimum in any one service. How will you navigate the change? Strategize key changes because some may even require a full stop.

As you plan for worship, consider planning a musical *prelude*. A prelude is usually music that's played at a soft level while people are entering the sanctuary. When done tastefully, a prelude can prepare people for worship by establishing a prayerful atmosphere.

You may also want to plan a *postlude*, which is music that is played or sung while worshipers exit the building. Look for words and music that reinforce the thrust of the message. At times the mood might be quiet, at other times joyful and exuberant. Some churches have a practice of inviting worshipers to come forward to the altar area in response to the message. At such times, the right touch reinforces an atmosphere of prayer and gives people vocabulary in expressing their consecration to the Lord.

A THEME FOR THE SERVICE

Sometimes the theme for worship is dictated by the church calendar. For example, at Christmas, Easter, or Thanksgiving, the theme is self-evident. But usually leaders seek the Lord for a theme for a worship service. Occasionally a certain Scripture will strike you and provide a general focus for worship.

Sometimes a theme doesn't emerge until the service is in progress. In the middle of the worship service, you may suddenly realize that a certain idea keeps coming up. You may even choose to express it verbally so the congregation becomes aware together. You might express it by singing a certain line repeatedly or by offering a pointed prayer.

Sometimes the pastor's sermon topic can help provide a theme for worship. That theme may not surface in every song but might be strongly present in at least one song. It's always wise to consult the pastoral team prior to planning the set list, to see if they have suggestions or preferences for the worship service.

Not every worship service has to have a theme. In fact, it's possible to labor so hard at crafting a theme for worship that the service can become labored and contrived. A worship service is simply a love dance between the Bridegroom and His bride, and love doesn't require a special theme. Love just wants to be expressed and exchanged. Worship is mostly about love. You can hardly go wrong by simply making corporate worship an easy exchange of affection and adoration. Whether or not a theme emerges, we're going to enjoy the presence of Jesus.

RUT ALERT

Be creative in providing variety in worship. If worship becomes too predictable, the people will lose interest and disengage. Since it's a living thing, love should be fresh and spontaneous.

There are almost as many different styles of worship as there are churches. Regardless of our form, we all fight the tendency for our form to become a rut. When we're in a rut, worshipers tend to go into autopilot.

Here are some rut-alert questions that can help us discern whether we've fallen into a worship rut.

1. Am I too easily distracted by horizontal dynamics around me? When we're in a rut, we tend to lose our fixation on the beauty of Christ and get distracted with the people dynamics in the room.

2. Does worship rarely surprise or intrigue me? God is full of surprises, but ruts are comfortably predictable. Nothing unexpected happens in a rut.

3. Has my language of worship become stale? Ruts are repetitive and don't require mental engagement. If a certain song is so overly familiar to the congregation that they can sing it without thinking, we might want to shelve the song for a season. Come back to it in a year or two and there will likely be new freshness on it.

4. Are most of the congregation not engaged with the worship? If worship no longer stirs us, perhaps we need help out of a rut.

5. Do I find myself silently predicting what will happen next in the service? That's one way my rut detector alerts me.

6. Is everything about our services smooth? Ruts are smooth. Smooth services can coast right past the Holy Spirit. To get out of a smooth rut sometimes requires something dramatic, even jarring.

7. Do new approaches to worship bother me? If a change in style of worship seems off-putting, maybe I'm clinging to the overly familiar and need help to climb out of a rut.

8. Is the time allotted to worship getting shorter? When we're in a rut, none of the bored worshipers feel deprived when the worship is cut short.

9. Do visitors struggle to connect with our worship style? Ruts tend to become ingrown and lose their relevance to guests and visitors.

Once we're aware of the ruts we're inclined to fall into, what can we do to avoid them?

KEEP WORSHIP FRESH

I encourage worship leaders to intentionally introduce variety and creativity into corporate worship. We want our services to be alive, breathing, engaging, even provoking. Mind if I share a few ideas on how to do that? Not that I mean for your creativity to be limited to my ideas, for creativity has no limits. Simply view my prompts as helpful ways to get started in the quest for Spirit-inspired worship services.

1. Fresh start

Start the service in a way you've never done before. Have everyone stand and introduce themselves to someone nearby they don't know. Read a Scripture. Begin with a prayer. Do not begin with a prayer. Suggest a theme for the worship. Have a time of silence. Show a brief film clip. Let the first song be instrumental only, while everyone remains seated. Start with Communion. In other words, start with something unexpected.

2. Go acoustic

Occasionally have the congregation sing without musical accompaniment. Or do an entire worship set with just one acoustic instrument.

3. Select a group

For a certain chorus, ask that it be sung by men only. Or by women only.

4. Kneel

Invite those who are physically able to go to their knees when the moment is right.

5. Change the order

If your service tends to have a certain order, change it up some Sunday. For example, start with the sermon and end with worship. Let worship that week be a response to the message.

6. Move the furniture

Lead worship from a different spot. If you typically stand in the center of the platform, move the team around and lead from one side of the platform. Or come off the platform and lead from the altar area, or the front row. Have the worship team turn their backs to the congregation and face forward, with everyone else, toward Jesus. I once visited a church in New York City, and when the worship launched, I could hear the voice of the leader but couldn't figure out where the leader was. After looking around for several moments, I finally spotted the pastor, standing in the front row of the congregation with a mic, facing the front, and leading the song. Nobody paid him any attention because the people's hands and faces were raised and their hearts were centered totally on the Lord. For me, that moment was very refreshing.

7. Go listless

Tell the congregation you're about to do an entire worship service without any known songs. Let it be a service in which we sing Scriptures and spontaneous chorus lines and spiritual songs, offer prayers, worship quietly, and meditate. Who says we have to sing hymns in order to worship? *Spiritual songs* (Eph 5:19; Col 3:16) especially invite innovation. Spiritual songs are spontaneous expressions of our spirit that are improvised in an unrehearsed, unpremeditated manner. The endless possibilities within spiritual song are like a blazing universe awaiting our exploration. (Refer back to chapter seven for more on this.)

8. Change music styles

Practice a song that has a music style totally different from what your church typically uses. Does your church sing classic chorales? Caribbean salsa? Country? Rhythm & Blues? Opera? If not, go there. Occasionally add the spice of a song in a minor key. Solomon once wrote, "Have you found honey? Eat only as much as you need, lest you be filled with it and vomit" (Prov 25:16). *Sweet* worship is *sweet*, but too much sweet is nauseating. Mix it up. Worship has room for diversity—from warfare to waiting, from shouting to silence, from exultation to exaltation.

9. Communion

Creative approaches to the Lord's Table can infuse fresh meaning into Communion. It can be administered in countless ways. A different theme and Scripture can be emphasized each time. If you usually do it every week, skip a week. If you usually do it once a month, do it weekly for a month. Have the people come forward; serve them in their seats; have them exchange with a neighbor; let the children serve the supper.

Make it an opportunity to pray for one another. Put it in a different place in the service order. If Communion usually happens before the sermon, do it after the sermon. If it typically happens after worship, do it in the middle of worship. Or plan the entire service around the table, with the Lord's Supper being the apex of the meeting. Ask the Holy Spirit for guidance on ways to keep Communion fresh.

10. The offering

Furthermore, be creative with the offering. If your church doesn't normally do a collection but receives gifts in a box in the back, one Sunday do a collection. One week have the worshipers place their gifts on the platform floor. Start the service with the offering. End the service with the offering. Put the offering and Communion together, with everyone bringing their gift then receiving Communion. Use preaching, Scripture, and song to make the offering the culmination of the meeting. Always ask the question, *what can we do to freshen up the offering time so it remains a meaningful, heartfelt expression of worship?*

11. Sing Scripture

There's room for so much innovation in the singing of Scripture. One of the most powerful ways to make worship creative is to encourage people to sing while their Bibles are open to a Psalm. Try it sometime. While singing a song that everyone knows, also encourage them to open their Bibles to a verse, and let that verse intersect with the lyrics of the song. The lyrics mixed with the Scripture can take a worshiper's heart to new levels of devotion to Jesus. Place the verse on the screens for those with no Bible.

12. Sing our own song

Train your congregation to become verbally articulate in worship. In other words, help them say more to Jesus than just the lyrics projected on the screens. Suppose every time I wanted to say something endearing to my wife I pulled out a Hallmark card and read its poetry to her. She would probably stop me eventually and say, "That's very nice of you, dear, to say those sweet things to me—but now, how do *you* feel about me?" Singing the lyrics on the screen is like singing from a Hallmark card to God. It's nice, but He wants more. He wants to hear from each of us in our own individual way. Encourage and coach worshipers to learn to express themselves to God in their own heart language.

Worship is loving and communing with God. I don't mean for my suggestions on creativity to complicate that simplicity. I only want to help us recognize and escape from predictable ruts. Several times the Psalms exhort us to sing to the Lord a *new song*, because He wants our romance to always remain fresh and adventuresome. Steer free of stale rituals. We want to do more than stay with the comfortable—we want to invest the effort to keep love alive and vibrant.

SING A NEW SONG!

The Psalms repeatedly exhort us to *sing to the Lord a new song* (Ps 33:3; 40:3; 96:1; 98:1; 144:9; 149:1). Clearly, the Lord delights when we bring innovative and creative expression to worship. But it's not simply for the sake of novelty. New songs help keep us from those ever-encroaching ruts. Fresh language and a new tune do something to awaken and rekindle the flames of love. Additionally, let me mention a couple other benefits of new songs.

New songs force us to think. It's easy to disengage mentally with familiar songs, but new songs grip our minds and hearts in new ways. And when we're more engaged in truth, worship grows deeper.

New songs expand our vocabulary of worship. Every song a church learns equips it with a greater breadth of expression. Sometimes a worship leader will want a song that expresses a specific theme, and they'll launch a search to find the right song. The more themes our repertoire covers, the fuller our worship can become.

A new song is a response to something new God is doing. Has God done something new in your life? Write a song. Has He done something new in your church? Write a song. Is God emphasizing a certain topic to your church through the current sermon series? Write a song to support that emphasis. Something galvanizing happens in a local church when they sing songs that were birthed in their own church family.

For more on the power of new songs, see my book, *FOLLOWING THE RIVER: A Vision for Corporate Worship*.

PURSUE NEW SONGS

Worship leader, I encourage you to pursue new songs in two directions. First, identify the best new songs that are being produced by the body of Christ globally, and use them in your church. Find ways to keep new songs coming across your screen. We want to be singing the songs the global church is singing in this hour.

And second, reach toward the goal of crafting new songs in your local church. I believe God wants to give your church its own sound. Some of today's leading songwriters have songwriting tips posted on YouTube.com. Share the best clips with the songwriters in your church. Help them unlock what's inside.

Experienced songwriters can teach you how to collect song ideas. You might have a brief line that you know is strong but don't know what to do with it. Hold onto it. Memorize and save it. One day that little line might help to finish a great song.

Collect melodic ideas, and then incubate them. Eventually, the idea could grow into a song, or could fit into another song you're working on. Or you may find another songwriter with whom you can collaborate and put your ideas together. Some of today's best worship songs came together through the collaboration of two or more songwriters working together.

Incubation is sometimes followed by inspiration. In one moment, a line you've incubated for months can suddenly explode into a bigger idea—opening into an entire song right before you.

Inspiration is often followed by revision. Now that you know you've got an entire song, the whole thing is examined and revised. Every word and note are scrutinized. Can it be said better? Can the melodic hook be strengthened?

Not all songs are written through inspiration. Some are written through determination and discipline. Sometimes the pressure of a deadline helps us write.

Seek to write songs that others want to sing. It you're the only one who likes to sing your songs, you might want to hone your craft and learn how to write songs that a general audience connects with. Cultivate your art. Grow your skill.

Many churches hold songwriting retreats for all the song-writers in their church, to inspire and invest in them. Groups of songwriters will collaborate on new songs together and plan to bring home with them several new songs for their church to learn.

SONG ELEMENTS

As you write new songs, here are some elements to consider.

1. Singability

Is the song easy and fun to sing? Are the melodic inter-vals between notes easy to navigate? Creative rhythms make a song interesting, but if the syncopation is too intricate, it can become difficult to sing.

2. Melodic hook

Is there something catchy about the melody? Strong songs have a melodic hook that stays with people. When a song has melodic grab, people will find themselves singing that line throughout the day. Are the chord changes smooth and interesting? Is there a satisfying sense of finality at the end of the song?

3. Message

Does the song actually say something? Does the music reinforce and support the message? Do both words and music join together to communicate one message? The mood of the music should match the temperament of the words. The highest note in the melody line should reinforce the most important idea in the song. Don't try to say too much with any one song but limit yourself to one basic message. Most popular hits can be summarized in one word or one key phrase. Make the main idea of the song easy to spot.

4. Words

Use familiar phrases and expressions, but avoid clichés. Select stimulating words that evoke strong mental images. If two words can be used to say the same thing, choose the more colorful word.

5. Repetition

Look for ways to repeat strong melodic ideas, powerful lyrical concepts, and solid chord progressions. It's possible to put too many musical ideas into one song. Make it strong and then keep it simple through repetition.

6. Rhythm

It's important how you align words with the meter of a song. The emphasized syllable of a word will usually fall on a strong downbeat. For example, suppose a line in a song says, "the *name* of the *Lord* is to be *praised.*" The italicized words in that line would typically coincide with strong down beats in the song.

Okay, enough from me on songwriting. I'm the guy giving advice on songwriting who's never had a song go viral, smile. So let's listen to someone who has. Turn the page and let's learn from someone who's seasoned in songwriting—Bryan Torwalt. Thanks, Bryan, for writing this next chapter.

CHAPTER 11

SONGWRITING

By Bryan Torwalt

Bryan and Katie Torwalt have been songwriters and worship leaders for over ten years and have been part of the Jesus Culture
Music label since 2010. Bryan's passion is to see the church encounter God through worship. Writer of the Grammy Award-
winning song, *Holy Spirit*, and *When You Walk Into The Room*,
Bryan is committed to continuing to craft songs that help move
people forward in their journey with Christ.

I get this all the time—someone comes up to me and
eagerly starts the conversation by asking, "Have you heard
this song yet?!" There's more buzz today than ever over new
songs because music is such a huge part of our culture.

Songs are powerful. A song can awaken nostalgic memories from a season in our past. Songs can comfort us in times
of sorrow and loss. They can pull us from despair and bring
us back to hope. Once you know a song, you'll probably remember it for the rest of your life. Songs actually have the
power to shape culture and beliefs.

Growing up in church, much of what I learned about God
and the life of faith came through the songs we were taught.
I even learned the books of the Bible with a song! Whenever

I'm writing a song, I'm always aware of the potential power of the process before me.

What an incredible time to be alive—when the release of life-changing songs is increasing exponentially. Songwriters are springing up everywhere, giving language to what God is doing in believers everywhere. Some of these songs are sweeping through the global body of Christ and out to the ends of the earth. New songs are giving fresh language to ancient truths and awakening our longing for Jesus.

MY JOURNEY

Let me introduce myself a little bit. I started writing songs while in high school. Although I loved the presence of God, back then I wrote songs mainly for girls. I wasn't a great musician, and honestly I'm still not that great, but I loved picking up the guitar, playing the few chords I knew, and creating my own words and melodies. It was an incredible feeling to listen to a recording of a new song that somehow came out of me.

As I began to write worship songs, I struggled to frame meaningful lyrics. It seemed like everything I wanted to say about God had already been said. But I loved to worship Jesus, and I just kept at it. I'd close myself in my room, strum two chords back and forth on the guitar, and sing the simplest lyrics and melodies. Sometimes I'd feel His presence in powerful ways, but when I'd go to write or record the song, it would feel so unoriginal that I would throw it away.

There were probably a lot of bad songs in my earlier days, but looking back now, I realize how honest they were. The song was cultivating my heart. I also noticed that the songs that were meaningful to me were starting to have the same effect on others.

After I married my amazing wife, Katie, we became worship pastors at a small church. After leading what seemed like the same songs every Sunday, Katie began to suggest we could write worship songs, too. That's where it started for us—we began to write songs together for our church. And for an audience of One.

The songs were simple, but they were bold and honest songs to God. It wasn't until we were really involved in the church and gained a heart for the church that the songs really began to flow. You don't need to be on staff at a church to write worship songs, but I do think you need some of Jesus' zeal for the church. Something happened in me when I saw authentic hunger in people's hearts during worship. For me, leading hungry believers into the presence of God never gets old.

ONE VOICE

Almost every time we introduce a new song at our church—Jesus Culture Church in Sacramento, CA—we watch as it galvanizes and unifies the believers in their love for Jesus. New songs allow us to put language to our own personal experiences, but more than that, they tell the story of our community of faith.

I encourage every church to cultivate the songs of their own community. Something beautiful and releasing happens when believers begin to sing the songs of their own journey together. It's personal. And something that's personal for you is often significant for others as well.

We've been extremely blessed by the Lord's grace that has enabled us to write songs that have been received warmly and sung widely by many other churches. The song, *Holy Spirit*, got covered by multiple artists and even won a Grammy Award. That song was on our first album in 2011, and get this—we wrote all the songs on that album while in the anonymity of a small church in central California. Back then, we had no idea God was going to take the songs that small congregation loved and export them to the world.

I encourage you, therefore, to write the songs. God can find a David in any remote place of the earth and carry the songs on the four winds. He can find a song anywhere!

STEWARDING THE GIFT

I find it challenging to stay fresh in songwriting. Once a song has had some level of success, I'm tempted to go back and copy that same sort of thing. But I must keep moving forward. I want my relationship with Jesus to be alive, and I want the songs that come from that relationship to be alive.

After finishing our first album, Katie and I took a break from writing for a while. A few months later, when I started to sit down with the guitar again, I would get so frustrated with everything that was coming out. It's as though I had writer's block. After ten minutes in my room, I'd throw my guitar on the bed and walk out feeling defeated and discouraged. Growing desperate, one day I asked God for breakthrough. Suddenly, it seemed like the Lord said, "Maybe if you would sit on an idea, and work on a song for more than ten minutes at a time, it would turn into something you actually liked."

When I think back to that moment, it always makes me laugh. That word was simple, but I really needed to hear it. Was I expecting God to sovereignly download songs to me? Did I think I could bypass the grueling process of finding and excavating the song that was deep on the inside? Here's my point. God took me on a journey to find and develop a process for songwriting that works for me, and I'm persuaded He'll do the same for you.

Let me share a couple more things from my experience.

COLLABORATION

Katie and I co-write virtually all our songs, and along the way we've learned to dance more smoothly together. There's no single formula to writing a song. Each song happens uniquely and differently. The more you write, the more your approach will vary.

Get ready to write bad songs—lots of bad songs. You'll work hard on them and then toss them. But the more bad songs you write, the better your chances of writing good ones.

I have a love/hate relationship with co-writing, smile. Something I love about co-writing with Katie is that I have a level of trust and vulnerability with her I don't have with anyone else. Our process is helped by being honest with each other and gleaning from each other's ideas.

In recent years, we've done some writing with others as well. We've written with our heroes, our friends, and even with some people we had never met before. For example, our record label set up a week for us in Nashville during which we had two or three writing sessions a day. It was exhausting! It was our first time to be with some of our co-writers, and it felt like a bunch of blind dates jammed into one day. The schedule was packed and challenging, but we learned a lot that week. With some of our co-writes we had an instant connection on such things as lyrical content, melodies, style, and taste. With others, we worked hard and got nowhere. We learned that you'll hit it off great with some writers and not with others. And it's okay.

More and more songs today are being written as collaborative endeavors. Something I value about writing with others is that we're all stretched as writers and humans. We learn from each other's experiences. Their process of how they interpret something, turn it into lyrics, and tell a story is often very different from mine, and yet we find that we're stronger together. I bet you can write some really good songs on your own; but if you'll push past the awkwardness and challenges of working with other writers, chances are you'll come away with some *great* songs and also fabulous relationships.

INSPIRATION

When we're asked about songwriting, one of the most common questions is about our inspiration. How do we come up with song ideas, and how do we turn the inspiration into lyrics and a story? To be honest, I don't think we're the greatest storytellers. One of my favorite songwriters is our friend, John Mark McMillan, who is perhaps best known for his song, *How He Loves*. His songs are filled with beautiful metaphors and brilliant stories. Katie and I tend to be more straightforward with our lyrics. Either way, it needs to come from the heart.

We've learned to just sing and express what we're feeling and thinking in the moment, even when it doesn't come out perfectly. We get it out there and then go back and work on it. Almost nothing comes out finished and polished the first time.

Keep collecting your song ideas, no matter how inspired or uninspired they may feel at the time. Here's how it works for us. Sometimes, when we're together such as in the car, Katie will start to sing a melody that I think is cool or catchy and I'll pull out my iPhone recorder and capture the lines. Later, scrolling through my old voice memos, I may come across an incomplete song from months earlier. Since I'm in a new place personally, it can spark something entirely fresh for me. I'll suddenly discover God is speaking to us in a fresh way using something that was recorded months earlier. I'm never afraid, therefore, to tuck something away for the time being and return to it later on.

Some songs take longer than others. Our song, *God With Us*, is an example of a song that took us a long time to finish. It began when our best friend's three-week-old daughter, Penelope, contracted bacterial meningitis. The diagnosis of the doctors was grim, so it was scary for all of us. Katie and I were taking a break from travel, so we were able to spend a lot of time with them at the hospital. One night, Katie came home from the hospital and said, "While I was praying over Penelope, I got this chorus. Maybe we could write something around it." The chorus was simple: *God with us, God for us, nothing could come against, no one could stand between us.* That message was something we all needed in that moment. We sang it with confidence. To the amazement of the doctors and to the praise of God, after a month in ICU Penelope ended up recovering completely!

That chorus was very personal to us because of Penelope's story. Any time we'd try to write a song around it, we couldn't find words to match our feelings and gratitude to God. The story meant so much to us that we were ready to wait patiently for the right words to match this precious, simple chorus. When the verses and bridge finally came, it quickly became one of my most favorite songs. For the first few months, I cried almost every time I sang it. I'd be honored if others would want to sing it, but to be honest, that's not really what I care about. It's meaningful to me, even if nobody ever sings it. It marks the story of God's manifest faithfulness in the lives of our best friends, and no one can take that from us.

Here's my point. Find inspiration in your life and journey. Find it in your community and family, write it in honesty, and then sing the story.

ORIGINALITY VERSUS ACCESSIBILITY

Katie and I have wrestled over the years with the tension between originality and accessibility. Originality is the quality that makes our songs unique, carrying the distinctive fingerprint of our creative touch. Accessibility is the quality that makes a song easy to enjoy, easy to relate to, and easy to sing over and over. A song is proven to be accessible when the wider body of Christ picks it up and sings it enthusiastically.

On the one hand, you can so be yourself that nobody wants to sing your song. On the other hand, you can write songs that are easy to sing but also just a cookie-cutter reflection of the stuff everybody's producing. I don't want either extreme. I want to be original and true to myself, but I also want to write songs that connect easily with the whole body of Christ. It's a tension that we manage.

You have your own personal history with God, and the more you rely on that in the writing process, the more authentic your worship songs will be. Ground yourself in good theology, meditate in the Scriptures, read other books that will ignite your walk with God, and you'll write with originality.

But you also want accessibility. Accessibility means people are moved by the song, connect with it, and enjoy it. When people want to play your song hundreds of times, you've made the song accessible. Sometimes, in the middle of the week, I'll find myself still singing or humming one of the songs from the Sunday set list. It was written so skillfully that it finds easy access to my inner song.

After all, this is the goal of all songwriters. While we want to be authentic and original, bottom line we want you to get our song stuck in your head. We want it accessible.

IDENTITY

The last thing I want to say on this topic may not seem very practical to you, but it has everything to do with songwriting. Creatives struggle with insecurity. We become so attached to the songs we create that, when someone criticizes them, we take it personally.

God is perfect, and everything He creates is perfect, but that's not true of us. We're human, and our creations are flawed.

Learn, therefore, to be vulnerable by allowing others to speak into your work. Take the risk of writing with others. You'll profit from their input, and you'll grow. Let's find our identity in God so we can receive input from others without taking it as a personal attack.

Finding our identity is not a destination but an ongoing process. As we abide in Christ and live in His word, our identity in God is continually strengthened. The more confident we become in who God has made us to be, the more confident we become in what we do.

After fifteen years of songwriting, I've discovered that writing a good song doesn't validate who I am. My identity was purchased on the cross of Christ. I don't create to gain His approval; I create because I already have His love and acceptance, regardless of the quality of my creativity.

I'm going to keep writing bad songs that nobody will ever hear or sing. Haha! But I also know this: By the grace of God, there will be some good songs in the mix, too. Because I'm just going to keep on writing songs. At the end of the day, just doing it is what's going to make you a better songwriter. Grow in your theology, know your audience, don't be afraid to be vulnerable, lean on other people, and above all, *just keep writing.*

CHAPTER 12

HARP & BOWL WORSHIP

By Jaye Thomas

Jaye Thomas is a Dove Award-nominated singer, songwriter, teacher, and worship leader. His songs are featured on dozens of albums, and he travels extensively both domestically and abroad. Jaye and his wife, Nayomi, are founders of songofhopeministries. org and live in Kansas City, Missouri, with their three children Mahan, Justice, and Addison. He serves currently as Director of Forerunner Music Academy at the International House of Prayer (ihopkc.org).

My wife, Nayomi, lived in a few countries before settling here in America. Smart and well-travelled, she speaks multiple languages. And then there's me. I'm just an American boy from the south. While *southern* could perhaps be called a language of its own, there are really only two languages in which I profess fluency: English and Christianese. You probably know what I mean by *Christianese*—the language we believers speak when referring to all things Christian.

As a conference worship leader for more than two decades, I can't count the number of Christian events I've attended where the conference themes were so similar they almost became clichés:

Bringing Heaven to Earth
On Earth as in Heaven
Your Kingdom Come

What do these phrases mean? Usually they express a sincere desire for divine healing, miracles, and all that we mean by our designation, *revival*. Is this desire valid? Yes. It was Jesus Himself who coached us to seek these things:

In this manner, therefore, pray: Our Father in heaven, hallowed be Your name. Your kingdom come. Your will be done on earth as it is in heaven (Matt 6:9-10).

Based upon this prayer, therefore, we ask for *worship on earth as it is in heaven*. While those words might strike you as *Christianese*, they're much more than that. They represent an authentic cry for the kingdom of heaven to be manifest in our midst here on earth.

WORSHIP AS IT IS IN HEAVEN

When we desire worship on earth to reflect heaven's model, we need to know what heaven's worship looks like. How else can we imitate it here on earth? Thankfully, John gave us a glimpse in the book of Revelation of what he heard and saw when he was caught up to the very throne room of heaven. Look again at this amazing passage:

Immediately I was in the Spirit; and behold, a throne set in heaven, and One sat on the throne. And He who sat there was like a jasper and a sardius stone in appearance; and there was a rainbow around the throne, in appearance like an emerald. Around the throne were twenty-four thrones, and on the thrones I saw twenty-four elders sitting, clothed in white robes; and they had crowns of gold on their heads. And from the throne proceeded lightnings, thunderings, and voices. Seven lamps of fire were burning before the throne, which are the seven Spirits of God. Before the throne there was a sea of glass, like crystal. And in the midst of the throne, and around the throne, were four living creatures full of eyes in front and in back. The first living creature was like a lion, the second living creature like a calf, the third living creature had a face like a man, and the fourth living creature was like a flying eagle. The four living creatures, each having six wings, were full of eyes around and within. And they do not rest day or night, saying: "Holy, holy, holy, Lord God Almighty, who was and is and is to come!" Whenever the living creatures give glory and honor and thanks to Him who sits on the throne, who lives forever and ever, the twenty-four elders fall down before Him who sits on the throne and worship Him who lives forever and ever, and cast their crowns before the throne, saying: "You are worthy, O Lord, to receive glory and honor and power; for You created all things, and by Your will they exist and were created" (Rev 4:2-11).

Among the heavenly mysteries revealed here, we are made aware of the *eternal* nature of heaven's worship. One million years from now, we will be deeply engaged in a worship service that has no beginning and no end. If our worship on earth is to reflect this eternal reality, what does that mean for us? For starters, I believe it means that the days of singing three fast songs and two slow songs in corporate worship are coming to an end.

A model of corporate worship has quietly crept into the church in which we view worship almost like a multi-course meal in which the first course or appetizer is worship and the main course or entrée of the meeting is the teaching or preaching of the word. Said another way, we've conceived of worship as something that "sets the atmosphere for the word of God to be proclaimed." The heavenly model of worship, however, contradicts the notion that worship is a means to an end. In heaven, worship precedes nothing and stands alone. Glorifying God is revealed as an end all in itself.

Little wonder that heaven's worship is eternal. When we behold God in His glory, something spontaneous happens. Our hearts are awakened with fervent affection. There's something about gazing on God's glorious attributes that awakens in us a natural response of worship. To illustrate that, envision a campfire. Have you ever stood around a campfire for any length of time? Your eyes become fixated on the fire, and it becomes hard to so much as blink. Even conversations with those nearby become difficult because you're so fixed on the fire. Why? Because we were created to be fascinated by beautiful things.

Fire can be dangerous, but consider its beauty. It's constantly moving and taking new shape. In fact, it never takes the same shape twice. It's unpredictable. That's why we're naturally fascinated by its flames and can't look away. Scripture reveals that God is a consuming fire (Deut 4:24). Gazing upon Him is utterly captivating. *Forever.*

John said the four living creatures he saw were "full of eyes in front and in back" (Rev 4:6). This implies that their primary occupation is to gaze upon the Father in rapt wonder, and then their response, naturally, is to call out continually, "Holy, holy, holy, Lord God Almighty, who was and is and is to come!" (Rev 4:8).

What are they seeing? What causes them to say such things? And why is *that* their song of choice? I believe they cry *Holy* because each time they open their eyes they see a different aspect of who He is and what He's doing. They're enthralled with the beauty of Jesus! And it causes them to respond with the only word you can use when all words seem to fail: *Holy, Holy, Holy.* They're transfixed by the fire; they can't look away. And worship erupts from the depths of their beings effortlessly and reflexively. It's the only fitting response to beholding such beauty, and since the beauty is everlasting, so is the worship.

This description of heavenly worship is our model for worship here and now on earth. We long to gaze on the beauty of the Lord, be fascinated by His glory, and thus be empowered to worship Him night and day with the extravagance He deserves.

WORSHIP AND INTERCESSION

In recent years, the Lord has raised up many ministries that have devoted themselves to night-and-day prayer and worship. From many locations in the earth, worship and intercession are now ascending to the throne of God 24/7. I love it! One of those places is the International House of Prayer in Kansas City, Missouri, USA (referred to here as IHOP-KC). In 1999, IHOP-KC launched 24/7 worship in a prayer meeting that has continued unceasingly ever since.

At the time of this writing, I've been blessed to be a full-time worship leader at IHOP-KC for a decade. I've been thrilled to be part of this ministry in which entire worship teams minister to the Lord in two-hour sets, round the clock, offering the fragrance of spontaneous worship to Jesus in thirteen languages. Live streaming brings the prayer room to a global audience. It's a marvel to the global church and a testimony to the grace of God that IHOP-KC has been able to sustain this prayer meeting for so long.

IHOP-KC is one of the ministries that has made famous the expression, *harp and bowl worship*. At its essence is the idea of combining worship and intercession as we minister unceasingly before the throne of God. Let me explain.

In describing the worship of heaven, Revelation 5:8 says of Jesus, "Now when He had taken the scroll, the four living creatures and the twenty-four elders fell down before the Lamb, each having a harp, and golden bowls full of incense, which are the prayers of the saints." The living creatures and elders each had two things in their grasp: a harp and a golden bowl full of incense. The harp represented worship; the golden bowl of incense represented prayer and intercession. In their ministry before the Lamb, the living creatures and elders operated simultaneously in both worship (harp) and intercession (bowl). Hence the term, *harp and bowl*. It's pointing to the synergistic and catalytic power of combining worship and singing with prayer and intercession.

When God sovereignly called IHOP-KC to 24/7 worship and intercession, Mike Bickle (founder and director of IHOP-KC) realized, along with his small band of leaders, that they needed to develop a model for harp and bowl worship that would enable them to sustain 24/7/365 worship. The challenge was *sustainability*. How do you keep the song going when you have nothing more to give? Mike and the team realized they needed to develop a model that would keep the fire burning on the altar (Lev 6:13) when the meeting was "unanointed," boring, and nobody wanted to be there anymore. This was the laboratory that birthed the harp and bowl model for which IHOP-KC is known and beloved.

KANSAS CITY'S HARP AND BOWL MODEL

Let me explain IHOP-KC's harp and bowl model. A worship set typically consists of five parts: corporate worship, spontaneous singing in the Spirit, introducing a Scripture passage, isolating phrases, and then developing the passage through antiphonal song and spontaneous choruses.

1. Corporate worship

Most sets begin with a time of corporate worship. Songs from around the world are sung in this segment. New songs, old songs. We look for songs that are easily singable and promote a Godward focus. While it's not wrong to sing songs that look inward at our own brokenness and the things we desire from God, at IHOP-KC we seek to focus on the throne and on the attributes of God. To be sustainable 24/7, worship must lift our eyes to God. We might acknowledge our troubles, but we don't stay there. Like David, we return quickly to God's faithfulness in the midst of our troubles and trials. (For an example, see Psalm 3:1-3.)

One of my favorite things to do when leading in corporate worship is to be creative with the songs. For example, when singing, "I love You," I might change the wording to,

"We love You." Simple changes like this can lead a room of worshipers from being spectators to becoming participants. I also like to alternate new songs with old songs, all the while being careful to maintain a consistent theme. Some of the old hymns of the church (which are rich in theology and familiar to many) can be interspersed with new songs that have just been released. Creative measures such as these can galvanize corporate worship.

2. Spontaneous singing

After singing written songs, teams following IHOP-KC's harp and bowl model will then transition into spontaneous singing. In this segment, short phrases will often be repeated that focus on the nature of God. Often those phrases are based on a Scripture or a scriptural idea. Sometimes they will sing with spiritual language (other tongues). Here are three verses that support this kind of spontaneous song:

> I will pray with the spirit, and I will also pray with the understanding. I will sing with the spirit, and I will also sing with the understanding (1 Cor 14:15).

> Let the word of Christ dwell in you richly in all wisdom, teaching and admonishing one another in psalms and hymns and spiritual songs, singing with grace in your hearts to the Lord (Col 3:16).

> Speaking to one another in psalms and hymns and spiritual songs, singing and making melody in your heart to the Lord (Eph 5:19).

When Paul said, "I will sing with the spirit," I believe he meant he will sing in other tongues, and when he said, "I will also sing with the understanding," I believe he meant he will sing in his native tongue (such as Hebrew or Greek). Spiritual songs, therefore, can be sung in either your native language (such as English) or in spiritual language (other tongues).

What are the distinctives of psalms, hymns, and spiritual songs? In keeping with Bob's definitions in chapter seven, I would define psalms as the singing of Scripture, hymns as the singing of songs of human composition, and spiritual songs as spontaneous songs of believers in the moment.

Few churches typically have all three expressions—psalms, hymns, and spiritual songs—in their Sunday morning services. Most churches predominantly use hymns. As an example, Chris Tomlin's song *How Great is Our God* is a hymn, in the way I'm defining a hymn—a song of human composition. I love that churches use hymns so widely, but the Lord has led IHOP-KC to explore, in addition to hymns, the realms of psalms and spiritual songs. We do much singing of Scripture (psalms), and we explore spontaneous song (spiritual songs) every day of the week. I believe one reason the Lord has led us in these ways is so that we might help churches incorporate psalms and spiritual songs into their regular practices. It's really not that difficult, and in fact thousands of churches around the world are using spontaneous song in their gatherings in ways history hasn't seen before.

I've noticed that, when worship teams exercise themselves in the harp and bowl model, after a while spontaneous song becomes second nature.

Spontaneous singing can easily be incorporated into a song that's already known. After singing the English lyrics, the musicians can keep playing the same chords and melody of the song while the worshipers launch into their own spontaneous songs, all simultaneously, together with the worship team. Most spontaneous songs are short phrases that are repeated, and sometimes expanded upon. Worshipers will latch onto spiritual song best when they realize they can simply repeat one simple line. The phrase may reflect the subject matter of the song that was just sung, or it may reflect a Scripture. For others who have the freedom, they may sing in other tongues.

Singing spiritual songs in other tongues isn't a lofty spiritual place to which we must attain but is readily available to all who desire it. Otherwise, why would Colossians 3:16

command it? Every believer is able to worship in spirit and truth (John 4:24). Some believe that tongues shouldn't be sung or spoken in a public context, and I appreciate their position. But I see room here for differences of opinion. If someone speaks aloud in tongues in a commanding voice, and there is no interpretation, then I would consider that to be out of order. But if a group of saints, in a believers' meeting, sing in tongues together in the spirit of 1 Corinthians 14:2, I see that as a beautiful corporate song in the Spirit to the Lord.

3. Introducing a Scripture passage

Sometimes when a team is between two known songs, they'll pause and linger for a few moments around a specific verse. A certain thought or phrase might be sung by one of the singers, and then the whole team catches that phrase and sings it together. When singers are meditating on a certain Scripture, and they want to sing something based upon it, one of their goals is to sing it in a way that engages the whole room. We try to keep the spontaneous phrases that are sung simple and singable so that everyone can join in together. After that Scripture has been explored for a few minutes through spiritual song, we'll move into the next song that everyone knows.

Sometimes, however, when a worship team is following the harp and bowl model, they'll dedicate perhaps a half hour to singing from a specific passage of Scripture. Several verses of Scripture may be placed on the screens, and then the worship team will sing from that passage. Often the first step in this process is for one of the singers to sing through the entire passage while a chord progression is repeated by the musicians.

After the passage has been introduced in this manner, then the team will begin to *develop the passage*.

4. Isolating phrases

The primary way singers *develop a passage* is by *isolating a phrase* that is then explored. They will begin to sing phrases from the passage, along with spontaneous phrases that the Scripture inspires, all the while searching for a phrase that can be isolated for development.

As phrases are sung spontaneously, it will often become apparent that one of the phrases being sung has extra energy or clarity on it. This phrase is isolated by repeating it. At first, that simple phrase is repeated a number of times. Then, the singers look for ways to develop the phrase with related ideas. In this manner, a Scripture is excavated from every conceivable angle. Verses from other passages of Scripture may come to mind and get pulled into the mix. Some of our most delightful moments at IHOP are when a team begins to develop a passage, the Holy Spirit breathes upon it, and the entire room lights up as the congregation enters into the song together.

5. Antiphonal song

Antiphonal song is usually expressed in two ways. First, a phrase can be sung by one group of singers and then repeated and echoed alternately by another group of singers. Another term for this is *call and responsive singing*. Essentially, singers reflect the same phrase back and forth between themselves. This kind of antiphonal singing was practiced in David's tabernacle and also in Nehemiah's day, as recorded in this Scripture: "And the heads of the Levites were Hashabiah, Sherebiah, and Jeshua the son of Kadmiel, with their brothers *across from them*, to praise and give thanks, *group alternating with group*, according to the command of David the man of God" (Neh 12:24).

The basis for this kind of antiphonal singing seems to have been the worship of heaven as Isaiah experienced it. Isaiah was caught up to the throne, and he saw the seraphim worshiping around the throne. Isaiah testified of the seraphim, "And one cried to another and said: 'Holy, holy, holy is the LORD of hosts; the whole earth is full of His glory!'" (Isa 6:3). The seraphim sing antiphonally, back and forth between each other, as they extol the holiness of God. It's a beautiful template that we're invited to follow—*on earth as it is in heaven*. What a delight to reflect the very worship of heaven!

Another way antiphonal song can happen is by the simultaneous singing of two different isolated phrases. Here's how that often comes about. The musicians will establish a certain chord progression and then repeat it over and over. While those chords are repeated, the singers will isolate a certain phrase and sing it. Then, as they develop the passage, later on another isolated phrase will be identified. Since both isolated phrases are sung to the same chord progression, their melodies are compatible. One group of singers might sing one phrase, and another group of singers sing the other phrase. At the same time. This provides interest, but more than that, it strengthens the momentum and intensity of the praises.

Antiphonal singing has an interesting history in my own spiritual heritage. Being a black believer, I grew up in a traditional, predominantly black Baptist congregation. As part of our standard Sunday service order, there was a designated time for what we called *responsive reading*. A leader would read a Scripture, and the entire congregation would respond in unison by reciting a pre-written response. I look back and realize this was a form of antiphony—a *call and response*. Later, when I encountered antiphonal singing in harp and bowl worship, I realized this was part of my spiritual heritage from generations past. During slavery, antiphonal singing was commonplace while slaves worked the fields. Most were illiterate, and antiphonal singing was used to teach biblical truth. So there, that's a piece of my ethnic history!

In the harp and bowl model, antiphonal singing often births what we've come to call *spontaneous choruses*. These are usually quite simple phrases with simple melodies that are easily repeated by the congregation. They rise to the top because of the spiritual energy or clarity they carry, and then when the entire room picks them up, the synergy produced raises the water level of intercession in the room. Sometimes these spontaneous choruses are memorized and later used by songwriters to craft powerful worship songs. I think this is what the psalmists of David's day must have experienced.

All of this is made possible by prophetic musicians who are skilled in their craft, listen carefully to the singers and one another, and serve in gracious humility.

To learn more about the harp and bowl model of worship, visit www.ihopkc.org. You can watch the 24/7 webstream of the Prayer Room and access a ton of resources.

As worship ministries, we have a door of opportunity before us today that I think is somewhat similar to the door that opened to John, who wrote: "After these things I looked, and behold, a door standing open in heaven. And the first voice which I heard was like a trumpet speaking with me, saying, 'Come up here, and I will show you things which must take place after this'" (Rev 4:1). I believe the Lord has so much more He wants us to experience with Him in our times of worship, but like John, we must accept the invitation. We're being invited to experience now, in a measure, what we will experience with Him in fullness forever. I felt like the Lord gave me a choice. I could sing popular songs now that have no eternal weight or value, or I could enter into the reality of eternity and truly experience what it means to worship here on earth as in heaven. I'm choosing the latter.

CHAPTER 13

USING TECHNOLOGY IN WORSHIP

By Joseph Zwanziger

Joseph and Tosha Zwanziger are worship pastors at The Father's House in Vacaville, California, where they lead over 100 musicians and singers at multiple locations. As songwriters, musicians, and worship leaders, Joseph and Tosha have released many albums including *Pursuit*. Joseph co-authored the book, *Lessons for the Worship Team* with pastor David Patterson. Parents of Cohen and Iver, Joseph and Tosha have a passion to train, equip, and release the next generation to use their creativity in the context of presence-driven worship.

Technology has taken congregational worship by storm! And our use of new technologies in worship is only going to grow. In fact, technology is advancing so rapidly that, by the time this chapter goes to print, it will already be outdated. To be as timeless as possible, therefore, the focus of this chapter will not be on specific technologies but on general, overarching principles.

The book of Psalms mentions instruments such as harps and lyres, but I've never used either one on my worship team. Times have changed. Today we use instruments such as drums, guitars, and keyboards. And to that we have added technologies—things like loops, multitracks, and click tracks (metronome beat). Even though the musical expressions of worship teams vary by culture and time, the heart behind it all remains true to the original Davidic calling of ministering wholeheartedly to the Lord.

Most churches today utilize technology in their worship services. At the time of this writing, multitracks have become a popular tool. What are multitracks? After recording a worship song, producers will assign the various vocals and instruments played to their own individual tracks. With a computer or other playback device, a worship team can select the tracks they want to use in a given song and then play along with them. For example, if a worship team has a strong bass player and electric guitar player, they can complement their sound by selecting the drums and keys and synthetic programming from the original recording—and even vocals—and have a full sound by playing along with the original tracks. Multitracks allow worship teams to supplement their sound with specific synth and rhythmic sounds that are nearly impossible to achieve with just the musicians on stage.

THE CASE FOR TECHNOLOGY IN WORSHIP

Proponents claim that multitracks have enabled teams to do what they couldn't do before. Critics argue that multitracks and other technologies can get in the way of authenticity in worship. The wave of the future, however, is on the side of technology. Each worship team must decide for themselves how they will use it to enhance corporate worship.

Colossians 1:16 says, "All things were created through Him and for Him." All things! Everything was created *through* God and *for* God. That includes all musical instruments and all styles of music. When rock-n-roll came on the scene in the 1960s, it launched a raging debate in the church regarding the use of things like drums and electric guitars in worship. These instruments were associated with secular bands like KISS (*Knights In Satan's Service*) that flirted with occult practices. The beat of the drums was thought by some to be demonic. "How could instruments used by ungodly bands *possibly* be associated with the house of God?!" Some believed the instruments themselves were evil.

Thankfully, though, those who knew better courageously brought these instruments into the church. God was glorified through increased musical expression, and the church today is better for it. I'm glad we didn't remain limited merely to the accompaniment of a piano or organ. Just as God is infinite, surely there are infinite means we can use to glorify Him and paint a picture of who He is to the world.

While we've progressed beyond the rock music debate, we face a new one today over things like lighting, video, synthetic instrumental sounds, and more. While many things can potentially distract, let's come back to Colossians 1:16 and remember that, "*All* things were created through Him and for Him." The questions for each church, then, are, *What should we use?* and *How should we use them?*

Here's my point. Technology is an appropriate tool for corporate worship when it's used, as Bob says in this book, to *provide the best possible opportunity for people to meet with God.* We don't worship technology. We worship Jesus, and technology is simply a tool to help.

BENEFITS OF TECHNOLOGY IN WORSHIP

Here are three benefits I see technology bringing to worship.

1. Increased musical expression

The use of multitracks, loops, or samples, etc., brings greater musical diversity to a team beyond what they can produce on their own. For example, if a team is weak in the areas of keys and synthetic drum loops, they can use those particular tracks from the original recording of a song and expand the sound of the team significantly—all in perfect pitch and time. As more technological innovations find their way into commercial worship recordings, multitracks can bring more of that original sound to the congregational worship experience, helping the song to "feel" like the version everyone knows. This actually enhances congregational engagement.

One potential negative is that worshipers can come to rely upon and expect the audio excellence of original recordings in church services. With care, though, we can help the people learn to worship regardless of the level of musical excellence. True worship is not reliant upon such superficial elements as technology, sound, or room temperature, but is focused on the *main thing*—God Himself.

2. Increased musical unity

Multitracks, loops, and clicks (metronome) are digitally generated, so they are in perfect pitch and time. They are a perfectly accurate "guide" a worship team can use to nail their rhythm and pitch. When used skillfully, they really augment a team's cohesiveness.

When I first started using clicks with our team, I started incrementally by using them only during rehearsals. After comfort began to grow, we started using them in fast songs during services, but not in slow songs so we could flow more easily between songs and spontaneous play. The final stage was using clicks for every song in every worship service. I was amazed how quickly our team became *more* comfortable using the click than *not*. Why? Because it made us more unified rhythmically. During musical crescendos, it's so easy to rush the timing—but the clicks cured that for us. Breaks and pauses all started again at the same exact time. Our sounds became more powerful, accurate, and expressive. Our fulfillment in our craft was enhanced. These little changes grew our confidence, emotional energy, and synergy as a team. And they had a strong effect upon the congregation, enhancing our collective fulfillment in ministering to the Lord.

Be on alert, though, for those unplanned moments when there's a technological glitch, and suddenly a song can become entirely unplayable (because the team is dependent upon a certain track sound). I've been in services where the technology malfunctioned and we had to throw out an entire song. Talk about distracting! Attentive worship leaders are always ready to flow with the unexpected.

3. Increased creativity

A great benefit of multitrack recordings is that they can give each musician a behind-the-scenes look into the songs they're playing. Each one can listen to the individual instrument they're playing from the original recording. The track functions like a tutor and helps the musicians become even more creative. For example, as a keyboardist practices their individual piano part, their accuracy improves and their proficiency grows.

By listening carefully to the tracks, musicians can learn from the best Christian musicians alive today. Professional musicians and producers labor over parts, voicings, effects, and the balance of the entire sound; I think we'd be wise to learn from them. Before you know it, your team will begin incorporating similar techniques into their playing. The creativity that's inside them will be unlocked.

MAKE TECHNOLOGY WORK FOR YOU

There's a steep learning curve when incorporating technology into worship services. The leader must master several programs and integrations, and then be able to troubleshoot when something goes wrong. If you're not guarded, you can find yourself serving the technology rather than it serving you. Here are some suggestions to make sure technology remains your slave and not your master:

1. Master the technology

As your team's tech leader, take the time to master the technology. Your diligence to do so will release and empower the entire worship ministry. If, on the other hand, we don't master the programs and integration, we'll be constantly thrown off and distracted from the things that are truly important—leading the congregation, following the Spirit, and unifying the band. Take the time. Master the technology. Make it work for you, not the other way around.

2. Define your purpose

Consult with the team and your pastor, and determine the role and purpose of technology in your worship ministry. Do you intend to use multitracks on every song? Why? Will you use multitracks only on special occasions for certain songs, or will you use them on a weekly basis? Here's why you want a practical philosophy for utilizing technology.

First, *your musical expression will be more effective* if you have a defined vision for *why* you're using it in the first place. For example, suppose a guitarist comes to your team with digital effects she's spent a lot of money on, and suppose you've chosen to build the sound of your team using analog pedals and amps. You would likely encounter some frustration because her sound would be in a different creative direction from your team.

Second, a defined purpose for the use of technology will *ensure you budget efficiently*. Insufficient clarity of purpose can lead to unnecessary purchases, and technology is usually not cheap! Don't purchase every interface, computer, or program—all the *bells and whistles*—you can find. Define what sound you're going for as a team, and budget your resources accordingly. Technology is a big investment, so spend wisely. Let's be good stewards of the finances allocated to our ministry. After all, those are tithes and offerings we're using.

3. Adapt to the setting

Be sure your use of technology is appropriate to your context. Is your vision for technology compatible with your pastors' vision for worship? In other words, do they support the way you use things like tracks, loops, and synthetic sounds? There will be constant tension and disunity in the team if your pastor "suffers" through worship and the worship team feels like they're being suppressed by their pastor. At all costs, strive for unity with your lead pastor. After all, unity leads to God's commanded blessing (Ps 133).

If you have three musicians on stage but the multitracks you use make them sound like a full orchestra on every song, does that *help* or *distract*? Answering questions like this will help you adapt technology to your setting. We want technology to be an aid—not a deterrent—to worshipers as they engage with the Lord.

4. It's a piece of the pie

Use technology for its strengths. Take advantage of its perfect pitch and timing. Introductions to songs will always be at the right tempo. It will broaden your team's sound. It's great to have technology on the team, so add it like you would add another member to the team.

And like every other team member, technology has its weaknesses. It can malfunction. It's insensitive. As already stated, we prepare to work with and around the limitations, rather than being held captive by them.

Worship clinicians commonly speak of *The Principle of One*. Let me explain what they mean. Imagine your worship team as a pie, with each member of the team representing a slice of that pie. When you put everyone's sound together, you want to end up with one complete pie. If certain members play or sing too much, and thus take up too much of the pie, you can end up with the sound of two pies. And that means we're overplaying the song. We want all the sounds to add up to no more than one pie.

When technological sounds are added to the mix, they take up part of the pie. That means we must create space in our sound for technology. For example, if a synthetic loop is added to the sound, then all the musicians must back off a little bit to make room in the total sound for the loop. Remind your team to play *with* the technology, not over it. There's a time for the musicians to give place to the technological sounds, and there's a time for the synthetic sounds to be diminished so the musicians can step forward.

5. Methods aren't sacred

Technology is a tool. We're not using it to look cool, but to enable the congregation to glorify God and exalt Him together. As already mentioned, the goal of worship leaders is to give people the best opportunity possible to worship the Lord. So if anything is hindering that, change it. Perhaps you've always done a certain song with multitracks, but in the next service you will intentionally do it with no tracks. Why do everything the same way every time? And if there are certain aspects of technology that aren't working for you, dispense with them.

NEVER STOP LEARNING

The members on my worship team have positioned themselves to be lifelong learners. I love that about them! In fact, this is a value that permeates our entire church. Who wants to hang around someone who thinks they already know it all? There's something attractive about people who are always learning, always pursuing new ideas, always striving for more. If professional musicians who are at the top of their craft practice for eight or more hours a day, shouldn't we also be pressing continually for more?

Smugness will hinder the flow of the Spirit and the creative life of your team. Allow the musical styles of your church to evolve as the culture of the global church evolves. When it comes to music, we never "arrive." Today's styles will be obsolete tomorrow. Worship leaders are musical pastors who shepherd the flock through incessant change. Furthermore, God's creativity never stops. To stay current with Him, we must be continually moving forward as we draw a broken world into His presence. When we remain lifelong learners, we attract new people, new ideas, and the new movements of the Holy Spirit.

God's on the move, music styles are moving, and technology is constantly changing. New innovations emerge every day! It's amazing how quickly yesterday's technologies become obsolete. Find ways to keep a pulse on what's happening in the world of music technology. How can you know if you want to incorporate something into your team if you don't even know it exists?

Even the channels of learning about the latest technologies are changing. Always be on the lookout for conferences, publications, and sites that will keep you informed. Learn from your friends who are a step ahead of you to help guide your learning process. Watch the trends. Ask questions such as, "How can this help to relieve burdens on my team?" "How can this expand our creativity?" "What are some new areas we can explore?" Never. Stop. Learning.

WHAT ABOUT LIGHTING AND VIDEO?

God created *everything* (Gen 1:1), and then He created us in His own image (Gen 1:27). Being created in His image means He has placed His own creativity within us. When we create, therefore, we reflect His character and image. So I say, let the painters paint, the artists draw, the poets write, and the players play. Make the video, paint with light, and glorify God with sound. Whatever we can do, let's do it with excellence and *make His praise glorious* (Ps 66:2).

Exodus 36:8 says, "Then all the *gifted artisans* among them...made curtains woven of fine linen, and of blue, purple, and scarlet thread." God has endowed artisans in every culture and time. In Moses' day, the artisans created with linen, wood, and more. In today's technological milieu, gifted artisans create with paintbrushes never seen before—things like video, lighting, graphic design, social media, applications, and more.

Since all things have been created "through Him and for Him" (Col 1:16), every new form of creativity has been given *by* and *for* Christ—to declare His character and glory to all humanity. *The highest expression of every form of creativity is found when making His praise glorious.* Lighting, video, graphics, and other "new" forms of creativity bring a breadth of expression to our times of worship that complement music and singing.

Worship isn't dependent on sound, video, and lights; but sound, video, and lighting exist to *enhance* the worship of God's people.

The question for church leaders, therefore, is not whether these forms of creativity *should* be used, but *how, when*, and in *what* context.

KEEP THE MAIN THING THE MAIN THING

Worship teams exist so that congregational worship becomes a time when we glorify God, make a place for Him to rest in our midst, lead people to Him, and follow His leading. Let's use every means possible to bring glory to God and see His people enveloped in encounters with Him.

Technology has opened a new season of creativity in worship that will continue to increase, but it must remain a tool and not become an end.

When I think of *keeping the main thing the main thing*, I'm reminded of the story behind Matt Redman's song, *The Heart of Worship*. Redman served alongside Mike Pilavachi (founder of Soul Survivor in the U.K.) as worship leader for the movement and their local church. At one point in the life of their church, they sensed that their congregational worship had become too dependent on external means such as instruments, lights, sounds, and lead singers. If the people liked the songs, they'd worship; if they didn't, they wouldn't. If the lights, sound, and environment were strong, they'd worship; if not, they wouldn't.

Realizing that worship had become too dependent on externals, Pilavachi decided to strip away all the lights, sound reinforcement, and instruments, and come back to the heart of it all—Jesus. In the midst of that return to the simplicity of worship, Matt found himself writing these lyrics in his personal prayer time:

> When the music fades
> And all is stripped away
> And I simply come
> Longing just to bring
> Something that's of worth
> That will bless Your heart ...
> I'm coming back to the heart of worship
> And it's all about You, all about You, Jesus
> I'm sorry, Lord, for the thing I've made it
> When it's all about You, all about You, Jesus.
> (*The Heart of Worship*, by Matt Redman)

He taught the song to their congregation with just his voice and acoustic guitar—no other supports. The simplicity of the song's message ignited the congregation because it expressed precisely what God was speaking to them in that season. As the church centered again on true worship, other instruments and sound reinforcers were gradually returned to the platform, and this time they didn't distract but enabled. They had returned to the heart of worship. From there, the song exploded around the world.

I pray that every church today would preserve this heart in everything we do—especially in our worship. We don't place our dependence upon the *tools* of worship, but keep our eyes centered on the *object* of worship—Jesus. There are other performing companies and touring acts that probably use technology better than us. But we have the unique privilege to partner with the Holy Spirit in glorifying Jesus, who said, "And I, if I am lifted up from the earth, will draw all peoples to Myself" (John 12:32). That's the main thing. Let's lift Him up in everything we do.

Books by Bob Sorge

Secrets Curriculum
- *Secrets of the Secret Place* (paperback & hardcover)
- *Secrets of the Secret Place: Companion Study Guide*
- Secrets 12-part Video Series
- Leaders Manual

Prayer

Reset: 20 Ways to a Consistent Prayer Life
Unrelenting Prayer
Illegal Prayers
Power of the Blood
Minute Meditations

Worship

Exploring Worship: A Practical Guide to Praise and Worship
Glory: When Heaven Invades Earth
Following The River: A Vision For Corporate Worship
Next Wave: Worship in a New Era

Enduring Faith

In His Face
The Fire Of Delayed Answers
The Fire Of God's Love
Pain, Perplexity, & Promotion: A Prophetic Interpretation of the Book of Job
Opened From the Inside: Taking the Stronghold of Zion
God's Still Writing Your Story
The Chastening of the Lord: The Forgotten Doctrine
The Cross: Never Too Dead for Resurrection

Leadership
Dealing With the Rejection and Praise of Man
Envy: The Enemy Within
Loyalty: The Reach Of The Noble Heart
It's Not Business It's Personal
A Covenant With My Eyes
Stuck: Help for the Troubled Home

For info on each title, go to oasishouse.com.

Bob's books are available at:
- Oasis House, 816-767-8880
- oasishouse.com
- christianbook.com
- amazon.com
- Kindle, iBooks, Nook, Google Play
- Audible

To stay connected:
YouTube/bobsorge
Instagram: bob.sorge
Blog: bobsorge.com
twitter.com/BOBSORGE
Facebook.com/BobSorgeMinistry

Another powerful Secret Place book:

A 20-day guide that helps believers become established in the building blocks of a consistent prayer life. If *Secrets* inspires you to pray, *Reset* gives the practical how-to tools to make it work every day. Only 80 pages.

Consider using *Reset* for
- Church-wide prayer initiatives
- Discipling new believers
- Small group studies

Check out PrayerReset.com for amazing quantity discounts so entire congregations can do this book together. Available in several languages.

PrayerReset.com